T0198645

CONCH SHELL
CONFESSIONALS

A Millennial's Memoir About
Sex, Love, AND Self-Discovery

DAX MARIE

authorHOUSE®

AuthorHouse™
1663 Liberty Drive
Bloomington, IN 47403
www.authorhouse.com
Phone: 1 (800) 839-8640

Published by AuthorHouse 01/23/2018

ISBN: 978-1-5462-2556-0 (sc)
ISBN: 978-1-5462-2554-6 (hc)
ISBN: 978-1-5462-2555-3 (e)

Library of Congress Control Number: 2018900866

Print information available on the last page.

This book is printed on acid-free paper.

EPIGRAPH

Because lord knows I need one.

•• ◉ ◉ ••

Ladies, this is a book about men (or maybe they could be more accurately defined as boys…little boys). So, if you have ever found yourself with the wrong guy (or guys as I have mistakenly done), I am so sorry. If you have ever had to deal with heartbreak, frustration, or immaturity due to boy-kind, I would like to apologize for their actions, too, because lord knows they never will. *Can I do that? Just apologize for the inferior gender like that? Oh well, I'm going to anyway.*

The dating struggle is real, and I feel your pain. Know that you don't stand alone in your dating of dipshits and DEFINITELY know that I understand (and that it's okay) if sometimes you're the dipshit because of the men you choose for yourself. As some cliché somewhere once said, you live and you learn.[1] So let's start making our way towards finding ourselves and learning about love. Oh, the happy struggles of vagina-hood.

Some of you men out there might be worried that you're going to show up in these pages. Some of you will be right—but not to worry my sweet boys, I have changed your names to ones that I find more befitting of you. So if you don't like it, I'm sorry, but you shouldn't have been so deserving of such colorful nicknames.

---

[1] Note: I've lived a lot and I'm still infantile in my learning. Patience, it's a virtue that I do not have.

GOOGLY-EYED

Yack, yack

There it was, the one-eyed monster, staring at me. Staring at my booze-ridden mouth, absolutely begging for me to put my smudged MAC-stained lips around him. In fact, he was pulsating at the anticipation of meandering into my moist wormhole. And that was the problem you see—he wouldn't sit still! It was as if he was mocking me, taunting me, challenging me—floating back and forth like he was on some gay[2] cruise ship. Waving at me as though I would never catch him.

Gotcha! Careful! Don't grab him too tightly. You can do this. You've done this a million times before. Well, not a million but somewhere up there—Dax, shut up and focus. Oh, right. That little cave weasel just kept slithering and wriggling in my hand, and I was starting to get frustrated. *Sit still, ya bastard.* Finally, I zeroed in on him, eye to eye, coaxing that flailing sausage in between my fuchsia fly trap (a.k.a. my mouth).

Suck suck suck. Suck suck suck. Suck suck suck. There I was suck, suck, sucking away, but the bed felt like a raft. It just kept going up and down...uppppppp and downnnnnnnn...uppppp and downnnnnnn. I felt like I was baby Moses floating down the Nile, only my basket was a bed (and it wasn't even my bed) and I definitely was not about to lead the Jewish people to freedom. *Stay focused. Just the tip. Yeah, just the tip. Ooh good, he likes that. Anddddd throw in a long lick. Perfect.*

My form was perfect. My lips consummately circular. My mouth, nice and wet. Nothing could go wrong despite the fact that the entire

---

[2] As in happy gay, not *gay* gay.

room was still moving. This was about to be my best one-night stand ever. I would make this John[3] guy my sex slave.

I was determined to finish him, but do you know how difficult it is to perform fellatio when all you can hear is the sloshing of booze in your belly? (Not to mention how loathsome the task is on occasion.) I think any and every well-marinated woman can attest: giving head is not always the most enjoyable experience. Especially when sex-deprived idiots push your head down toward their nether regions and insist on keeping their hands over your head, pushing you up and down on their flagpole.

Men, do you understand that your little member is a choking hazard?

I was going to town, really getting into it. Every now and then, when I could balance myself well enough, I would glance up to see his face. *Yup, he's digging it. You, Miss Thang, are a dome-dominator.* So far, this one-night standee was great. His junk didn't smell, it didn't taste weird (though my tequila breath could've neutralized it), and he was a freakin' babe!

But oh no, he had to go and mess that all up. What did he do? He did the one thing that would throw any woman off. No, he did not fart while I was down there. (I would've castrated him.) He pushed my head down so his little friend could go deeper into my mouth. *Hell no.* I forced my head back up. Then, he did it again. So I stiffened my neck and pulled my head up again. And again, he did it, and again I pulled myself up. This went on for a minute or two as I struggled to maintain my sex goddess mindset.

Finally, I got fed up, and, after nearly going a little too deep, I grabbed his hand and held it down. All the while, I continued my gracious gift without missing a beat. *God, that was annoying. Stupid, can't you tell when you're choking a bitch?*

You'll never guess what he did next. Anyone? Well, let me tell you— he enthusiastically whipped his other hand out of nowhere and squashed my noggin down while he launched his hips to the heavens. (Talk about

---

[3] Please note that I do not actually remember his name.

deep throating it!) I gagged. *Keep it in.* His hips remained up in the air (that motherfucker really didn't care), and his zealous digits tangled themselves in my hair while he continued the shoving of my face into his pubes. I gagged again. *Don't do it. Don't you dare do it.*

Suck suck suck turned into gag gag gag. There was no escaping his literal chokehold in my throat. I am not one for deep throating anything, and this fool was trying real hard to make me do so. He kept humping and pumping, and I kept gagging and choking (and silently dying). *Please keep it together. Please.* Hump. Gag. Pump. Gag. Hump hump. Gag gag. Pumpppppp. Yackkkkkk. Vomit. Everywhere. *Oops.*

Well, he stopped pushing my head down and, oddly enough, the booze stopped sloshing around in my belly (since it had all evacuated onto his dick). My eyes were brimming with tears as I gasped for breath. Upchucking left me feeling lighter and a lot less drunk, but infinitely more embarrassed. He wouldn't break eye contact with me. *Awkwarddddd.* Silence. No gagging, no slurping—just utter and pure silence filled his sexless room. He had forced me into giving bulimia a sexual connotation and now seemed upset about it. John finally broke his glare and began to examine the abstract expressionism (which is my favorite type of art) I had created on his junk. *Call me Upchuck Pollack.*

Finally, he spoke: "What the hell?!" I guess that meant he was not amused by the cocktail of añejo tequila and half-digested kale chips that now ornamented his once well-manicured pubes and kielbasa...my bad.

"Do you want a towel?" I asked.

"Gross."

"So is that a yes on the towel or..."

"What. The. Fuck." He groaned.

"Sorry?" I offered. I wasn't sure how seriously I should be taking his "what the fuck." *Hmm,* I received only a blank stare from purged-on-penis. So I decided to continue with my word vomit: "I mean it is kind of your fault though. You did push yourself way deep inside of my very sensitive throa—"

"Out," he cut me off.

"Should I help you clea—"

"Get out of my house," he interjected again.

"So you don't want my number?" I deduced.

"Outtttt!" His whole body shook.

I gathered myself, wiped the remnants of vomit from the corners of my mouth (onto his bed...*enjoy, bastard*) and put my sexy ass heels back on. Before I left forever, I decided I would try one last time to solicit myself to him:[4] "I'm on insta at Dax dot Marie. DM me." John[5] didn't say no...but I'm still waiting on that DM.

---

[4] Man, I really make myself sound like a ho.

[5] Note: I still don't know what the fuck his name was, so it is very possible that "John" DMed me and I didn't respond because he was uglier than the drunk me remembered.

●● ◉ ●●

DAYUMMM, WOMAN

●● ◉ ●●

They said pretty girls don't do those kinds
of things.[6] I told them to fuck off.

●● ◉ ●●

Confession (the first of many in this book): that didn't happen. I
didn't yack on some poor guy's little guy, which is odd considering
all of the drunken escapades I have succumbed to over the years. (I
say succumb like it's some religious experience.) So, John isn't real, but
that's not to say he isn't real for some other girl out there in this big,
bad world. Come on—this has to have happened to some drunk girl
somewhere. Whoever and wherever you are drunk, penis-puking lady,
I commend you.

Confession Number Two: I have never had a one-night stand, at
least not by its technical definition. God, I know…I'm so boring and
such a prude. Hardly. I have just never had the overwhelming and
insatiable desire to pursue a one-night-only romp. (I mean, I've stumbled
into one, but you'll read that later.) I'm sure they're exhilarating, but
I complicate everything as it is and I know I would twist the hell out
of a one nighter. So, my whole first chapter is a big, fat lie or perhaps
we could look at it as an imaginative rendering of a second date (which
you'll also read about later).

Right about now I'm sure you're wondering who the eff I am then.
I don't blame you; I would want to know who this lying chick is, too.
First, I am not a liar. I've just taken too many acting classes to count,

---

[6] VERY IMPORTANT NOTE: Don't ever let someone tell you how you should
   act. Be you!

and I love writing backstory. So lucky for all of you, I'm going to tell you all about me and my struggles to find myself in the millennial dating world. You're welcome, I guess.

I was born on a Sunday morning at 7:29 a.m. on July 26, 1992, in some beach town in California to Mama and my poor excuse for a Father (formally referred to as Assdrew in my house). My mother gave me the oh-so-holy name of Dax Marie.[7] The first few years of my childhood were a dream, and I was spoiled rotten with more love from my mother and, well, monetary love from my father than could be thought possible. I was Satan, tainted by the spoils of my father's uneducated, blue-collar success. The first five years of life were all rainbows and butterflies with wasted money flying left and right. Two more babies popped out of Mama's belly while Daddy Dearest popped a few more bottles at the end of each night.

Life seemed so great, but looking back, it was all just a big, fat cliché. Mama would cry and scream, the Drunk (aka the daddy who provided me with my issues) would throw shit then leave, frantically yelling some twisted amalgamation of dagger-like words as he ran out the door in an attempt to break Mama into a complacent housewife. It was like clockwork. He'd run off to his fat, crispy-haired mistress/secretary, whining through his drunken stupor about his dragon lady of a wife. But Daddy was the real monster and Mommy was weakened by confusion and sadness. We were just babies living under the horrid roof of a drunken imbecile.

Dumbass (I mean my farter—damn it, my *father*) came home less and less. Mama would never say what was going on, I just knew. I recognized the tragedy of it all—I knew our home was broken. Mama's thirty-year-old face was withering with every worrisome detail. No woman should ever have to deal with what she had thrown at her nearly every single day. As for us kids, we wanted Mommy and Daddy, but Daddy wanted drugs sprinkled with some rock n' roll. We craved his attention, screamed bloody murder at Mommy, and demanded with

---

[7] Confession: not my real name but the real one is so awful and common, I just can't bring myself to write it down.

fiery intensity to see Daddy, but not even Jesus Christ himself could bring such a damned man like that back from clutches of hell.

Eventually, my father disappeared completely, vanishing into the void that laid between his secretary's legs.[8] Though he would always manage to reappear when he had a pending court hearing to lower his child support. (Go figure.) For years this went on, this magic act of his. Disappearing into thin air and then reappearing when his narcissistic mother would tell him to do so. Unlike him with his magical little reappearances, the money—our money—completely disappeared.

My mother tried to support us as best she could, and as we all know, sometimes trying is not enough. Without Assdrew's cushy income, we lost our home. My mom managed to scrape enough money together to get us a bug-infested apartment nearby, in hopes of not changing our lives more than they already had. By then, Daddy Dearest had lost himself further to drugs and alcohol, but lucky for him, he always had his mommy to bail him out of jail and finance his habits.

As fate would have it, my mother could no longer afford our shitty apartment and our tiny family of four could no longer handle the stress of running into a drunk and drugged out daddy (since he loved to hang around the bars in our neighborhood). So by the time I turned eight, Nana, my mom's Colombian mom, opened up her tiny two-bedroom home to us. The four of us (my mother, brother, sister and I) crammed like sardines into Nana's second bedroom. The irony being that in that tiny house, in that tiny bedroom, we could finally breathe.

Nana saved us. She gave us a home but, more importantly, she gave us hope. When we moved in with her, I remember her telling me that this was our home now. She was a strict, yet silly woman. Her English was broken but that never stopped her from relentlessly teasing my whining baby sister.[9] Our house was full on female power—and of course, the super boy power of my brother. *Chant with me: ¡MUJERES!*

---

[8] That's called a vagina and she's called a homewrecker.
[9] She's probably the reason why I am such a smartass in Spanish. In English, I'm just really smart, like borderline genius.

¡MUJERES! ¡MUJERES PODEROSAS!!!! And just like that, life began to turn rosy again.

It was a Thursday in June, and we had been living in Nana's home for a year. My mother, brother, sister and I had just gotten home from school. Nana was sitting on the deep mocha and silky pink colored dining room chair facing the kitchen. She looked exhausted. My mother's body language turned to a mush of worry upon seeing her. I was nine and would do anything for this woman who had become my small family's saving grace. My task was simple: Nana asked me to get the mail. I walked out, grabbed the small stack of letters and ads and handed them to her. *"Gracias, querida,"* she hushed as she pulled the mail closer to her body.

Seconds. It was seconds later that Nana face-planted to the floor. Then everything seemed to swirl around me in slow motion: my mother as she rushed to Nana's side, my mom's voice as she told me to call 911, Nana's breathing, my brother's questions, my sister's tears, my mother's tears, my brother's tears, Nana's eyes tucked behind her eyelids, the fire truck, the police...the world. A stroke, the doctors would later diagnose. It was that one and then another that put her into a coma. A month later, Nana passed away on July 19. Her funeral was held on July 26—my tenth birthday.

Our life, which seemed to be finally falling into place, once again came crashing down. It was as though no one understood us. My dad's family was caught up in the oblivion of addiction and my mother's family was lost in the anger of death. Nana had been our hope, our lifeline, our love, and now it was as though we were all alone again. My mom would shed a tear or two out of frustration for her pained babies, sitting patiently, nurturing us until we stopped seeking the unsolicited love of a miserable man. She kissed our broken hearts, rolled pennies to feed us, loved us when no one else could understand our odd quirks and flaws and inspired us to dream big. The four of us, we made it through the worst of times and the worst of people and as a result, my mother, brother, and sister are my world.[10]

---

[10] Try to mess with any of them and see what happens...I'll maul you like a lioness protecting her cubs. (Yes, my mother can be my cub.)

As the years passed, I watched as Assdrew drank himself into a putrid grave of hatred and self-loathing, flowering it with methamphetamines. The only mourners of his self-destructing ways were (and still are) his sick, twisted mother and his self-deprecating sister. That drunk (and his entire family) is gone from our lives and we've all moved on. Every now and again, the old scars flare up, but what's the point of acknowledging such a pestilent nuisance? Life is a cliché and for nearly the whole of my own life, I fought against the world.

So, who am I then? After hearing all of these sad, tragic beginnings, I'm sure you think I am a mess. Truth be told, I am—kind of—but not in the pathetic way that you're probably thinking. I graduated from a big name university, I've had real "big girl" jobs but then quit them to pursue acting, and then took a break from that (since I wasn't getting real roles) to write. So, if it sounds like I have my head in the clouds and am "finding myself"—I am. But I would like to clarify that my personal goals have always been squared away. I know what it is that I want. I want to live a life better than that of my childhood and I want a man who completely loves and obsesses over me. Only that last one is a bit of a pickle: I never date a guy long enough to let him get close to me. So, there's the mess to be sorted. The question to answer, the problem to solve, the work to do. The story to tell—my indecision with men.

I know what I you're thinking: Daddy issues, right? Well, to that I say, "Let's not oversimplify." I never intended on being such a man-eater, though I suppose that's the very thing Freud was talking about when he condemned all females with "daddy issues" to be floozy miscreants. But this isn't Vienna in 1905. I am not a slut. It's such a harsh word and so misleading. And while we're on the subject, I'm also not a hussy, a harlot, a Jezebel, tramp, vamp, strumpet, trollop, or tart. I will accept vixen and offer extra credit for minx. (If this were 2005, you could call me a Samantha.) But what's in a name?

The answer is plain and simple: I made a New Year's resolution to "go bold" and bold I went.

Maybe this was all a mistake but the curiosity had to be broken, so I gave into a year of living boldly that never really ended. It kind of just caught on and stuck. I don't regret it, I love it, and some of my greatest realizations have come in the most unlikely of faces. I love men…is that so bad? But here's the bud of the bud: I'm not a man-eater. Well, at least not in the sense that you might think. You know the type to prowl from one man to the next—not that there's anything wrong with that. No, it was love and romance that I wanted. And once I got a taste of it, I'd put up with a lot more than I should have.

It's my nurturing mindset that I believe gets me in trouble sometimes. My I-can-save-your-damned-soul mentality. Believe me, I have met some "bad boys" in my day, and like the Florence Nightingale of dipshits, I always think, *I can help you…Let me kiss you back to health…Let me save you.* I used to think of this as benevolence, but now I know it's bullshit.

There are no bad boys, just lost boys. I am not Jesus and I cannot save any souls, no matter how hot they are. It's a lesson I've learned the hard way numerous times and I think I have only recently begun to understand it. So, I've grown up a bit, I guess. Learned a few things. And like I said, my greatest realizations have come from the most unlikely of faces.

So, yes, this is a book about love: hunting for it, chasing it, losing it, tripping and falling into it. And, yes, it's a book about sex: hunting for it, chasing it, losing it, tripping and falling onto…ahem…*it.* But more than anything, it's a book about self-discovery, navigating the learning curve of adulting, and learning the kind of tough lessons that only come when you have to pick yourself off the floor, block a guy's phone number (for the second time), and clean some curious stains off your dress.

I dove headfirst into love and sex, and, for better or worse, they have taught me that sometimes you just need to try the world on for size to really understand what it is you want and who you are.[11] So, here's my experience in the world of men.

---

[11] And sometimes you just need to get laid.

CHERRY POPPING GOODNESS

"Wait…I'm a virgin!"

It was the first day of June, summer was approaching, and I was about to leave my ignorant youth behind. Had I known what I was about to unlock, the never-ending battle upon which I was about to embark…I would have still made that decision, the whore-iffying one.[12] Prior to that youth-shattering night, I knew nothing about men and, truthfully, I knew far less about myself. Even more truthful would be me admitting that I slightly hated myself. Just ever so slightly. Okay, fine! I couldn't stand myself.

It had been a year since I had graduated from high school. Nearly everything and everyone I knew had been left behind. I had gone from being an International Baccalaureate student and varsity athlete to a student who had cheated on some data points in her senior year bio lab and tore her ACL in a matter of months. (I shall clarify now that schools are not messing around when they threaten to report your academic misbehaviors to *EVERY* university you apply to.) I had lost everything I had worked so hard for, and it was unbelievably frustrating and depressing. Despite my great GPA, a plethora of extracurricular activities, volunteer work and athletic participation, I was denied to *EVERY* single university I had applied to based on my ONE mistake.

ANGRY! I was ANGRY. I was depressed. More accurately, I was "lost all of my friends and ate my feelings and gained 40 pounds" depressed. I was inconsolable for nearly two years. That is, until one day

---

[12] Oh shoot, did I spell that wrong?

when I finally saw the silver lining. Seeing as I had lost "everything," what more could I lose if I went for it…the whole big dirty adult world? See, I had abided by a certain set of (religious) standards for nearly the whole of my adolescent life, and, as awful as this may seem to some of you, I decided *FUCK religion*. New Year's Eve of 2011, as I sat all by my lonesome self, I made a resolution that would forever change my life: GO BOLD.

My resolution served no purpose other than to free me from my self-inflicted shackles (I had bought into the idea that the Devil resided in the souls of the promiscuous). I wanted to try the world on for size. I wanted to get high, to experience the weightless burn of smoke in my lungs. I wanted to know what it felt like to be uncontrollably drunk and sloppy. I wanted to feel love and heartbreak and despair. I wanted to know the intimacies of sex. But more importantly, I wanted to shake myself free from the chokehold of depression that I had been judging myself into. So, I did it. I went BOLD.

It was my masterplan, *going bold*, and truthfully, it was a rather simple one. I was turning myself into a "yes" woman. I would no longer fake being busy as a means to get out of human interaction and would, instead, now make an attempt to be part of the world around me. In less than six months I had checked off most of my big list:

Smoke pot—check

Get drunk—check

Make amends with my father—check[13]

Sex—Where's that jingle-jangle at?

In all honesty, I was beginning to feel better…more human again. But there was still something missing: I was still a virgin. (Oh god, I make it sound like such a dirty word, *virgin*. Oh, the inhumanity!) I wanted to lose it so badly. The time had come for me to spread my legs and toss that nonexistent promise ring into the simmering abyss of Hades.

---

[13] Also to be noted that this was a short-lived amends because that dumbfuck done fucked up again.

I begged for it. Seriously, I *begged* my boyfriend for sex.[14] Pretty much gave him an ultimatum, in the kindest of ways of course, which is to say that I didn't tell him I was going to break up with if he didn't put out. *What's that saying that stupid high school boys use? Put out or get out.* Whelp, he wouldn't give it up, so I broke it off (the relationship, not his penis). So, I broke up with him and I set my sights for greener pastures and easier targets. Hello, skater boy (definitely won't be seeing you later boy).

Ever since I was a wee one, I have always had a thing for skaters. I blame my cousin. When I was about six and she was twelve, we would sit in my mom's bedroom hiding behind the blinds, watching the neighborhood boys skating in the street. And then, when one of us had finally mustered up the courage to shout out of the completely covered second story window, we would yell, "Hey cuties! What's your number?" So yes, it is all my cousin's (and possibly Avril Lavigne's) fault that I had, and still have, a thing for dirty skater boys.

It was only a matter of time before I tried to make my skating boyfriend dream into a reality—and by matter of time, I mean eleven years later. I was seventeen when I decided it was time to spread my wings (not my legs...not just yet) and get myself some of that cheddar[15] and hopefully a hunky street surfer. I had just gotten into a fight with my mom and marched my tear-stained face into the coolest skate shop I knew, mostly out of spite for the fight I had with her.[16]

"Is the manager here?" I demanded through muffled sniffles.

"I'm the manager," replied the short, good-looking man at the counter.

"Hi, I'm Dax. Are you hiring?"

"Are you looking for a job?"

"Yes, I want to work here," I said as though there was no room for his denial.

"Cool, come back here and I'll interview you."

---

[14] See, I went so far with human interaction, that I actually got myself a man...Well, he was more of a boy.

[15] That's street talk for m-o-n-e-y.

[16] Because that's what every rebellious teenager does: gets a job. (Note the sarcasm.)

In hindsight and with a few more years of knowledge under my belt, I now realize that this store manager was creepy and a little too touchy[17] and didn't actually want to hire me because of my abundant experience in retail, of which I had none. But that didn't stop me! I wanted that damn job and was naive enough not to be put off by my pervert boss (I mean, it's not like he was the last pervert I came across in a position authority). I killed the interview (which was bullshit) and got the job. I was now a bonafide skate shop employee. *Oooo, boys, come at me.*

This shop was the dive bar of skate shops, the Keystone Beer of skate shops, the Popov Vodka of skate shops, the Evan Williams Bourbon of skate shops. You get that it was shitty, right? One more? Two-Buck Chuck. Anyway, the owner was one of those fat coke heads who was snorting through the business funds, and the shop was taking a hard hit because of it. So, because of our lack of inventory, I didn't really get much action. I did learn how to skate though[18] and learned pretty much everything there was to know about skateboarding, so when the time came for me to impress a fella with my skate knowledge, I would be prepared. Yet, there weren't really any quasi-normal guys circulating through the store. I mean most of them were kids younger than me or just older weirdos stoned out of their minds. *Whatever.* It wasn't like I was going to die because of a lack of male attention. I barely knew how to talk to a guy I was so awkward.

As my seventeenth year came to an end, I was still chubby, a little depressed and overwhelmingly awkward, with no friends since I had spent so long hating the world. (This was pre-2011 New Year's Resolution.) Now, enter my first day of junior college, in the first classroom I sat in with a decrepit dictator of a teacher who assigned seating for us. *Uhh yeah, we're in college now, so is this, like, necessary?* To my right, no one, but to my left and one seat over—Hot Math Guy. He was twenty-four with bedhead and I was eighteen and primed to a tee. I was hormonal, pissy, and a real bitch.[19] I thought I was too good

---

[17] Not like rape touchy but like unsolicited massages brand of touchy.
[18] When I say, "learned," I mean I can stand on a board.
[19] Hey, this still sounds like the twenty-five-year-old me!

for everyone there. I mean, the only reason I was even at that school was because I got caught cheating on an IB Bio Lab and was denied by every university I applied to.[20] So, yes, I thought I was way better and way smarter than anyone and everyone in that dingy dump of a school…until I saw Hot Math Guy.

To be honest, at this stage in the game of love, he was just Math Guy. I didn't think he was cute when I first saw him. To be even more honest, I thought he was kind of ugly. That is, until I saw his shoes. No, they weren't Gucci or studded men's Louboutins, and they sure as hell weren't those antiquated puffy 90's skate shoes. Instead, my future cherry popper had the most erotic markings on his "hip" shoes—you might even call these hieroglyphics one of my love languages. His shoes were worn on the outsides from kick flipping, which meant he skated, which meant utter and total BAAAAAAABE. You bet your bottom dollar I wanted him now.

One semester, eighteen weeks, was all I had to try and get this man-boy to talk to me. He was such a hipster and I was so enamored and just like *sooooo* desperate for any male attention. But Hot Math Guy wouldn't give me the time of day. So young, so dumb was I, making comments under my breath in class, hoping he would chime in and talk to me. But alas, my efforts were to no avail; I was nothing to him. Until finally one day, about nine weeks into the semester, I'd had enough. I was determined to make HMG talk to me. So what did the pathetic, attention-starved, eighteen-year-old me do? I did the most logical (and creepiest) thing I could think possible while sitting in the middle of our algebra class:

"You skate?" I asked as I nervously fidgeted with my mechanical pencil.

"Huh?" HMG retorted, confused by my random question.

"Your shoes. You skate." I flicked my eyes down toward his feet.

"Oh, yeah."

I should've known he was totally not interested at this point but my teenage brain just thought, *winniiiiing!*

---

[20] Moral of the story? Don't cheat, kids.

"I work at [skate shop that I'm not going to name]," I confidently chimed.

"Rad, I've been there," he uninterestedly, yet politely responded.

"I could get you a discount," I lured him with the bait. *Bam. Got him.*

"Yeah? Do you have the new Janoski's?" he cooed.

"Yeah," I smirked.

"Cool," he nodded.

Bet you think he asked for my number...Wrong! He didn't make any mention of calling me or telling me when he wanted to meet up. He just left me on a high! I floated out of that classroom, trailing behind him as he walked to his next class, which just so happened to be in the same building as my next class. *Imagine that!* I thought that it would only be a matter of time before he asked me out since now he knew that I was a discount-wielding skate goddess.

Ugh, I was so naive.

The rest of the semester skated by and HMG never asked me out. We barely talked, but for some deranged reason, I still had it in my head that this man-boy would ask me out. I was absolutely convinced—but he never even took me up on my offer for an awesome discount. I never saw HMG around campus except for the two hours we had together in math class and the five minutes it took for us to walk to our next class—and that walk usually consisted of me trying to catch him as he bolted out of the room. *Hey, wait for me!* I was starting to think he was gay (which was my go-to anytime something didn't work out with a guy), until he finally did it. He who was the holiest of holies, in my own community college math class, asked for a discount![21] *Geesh, it only took ya all semester. Ah, who cares?!* I, Dax Marie, had done it! I cracked the code to Hot Math Guy's heart! And I sincerely thought that it would be all easy street from there. I was clearly an idiot.

Game time, baby. It was almost the end of our semester with just our final class left and Hot Math Guy had finally hit me up about my until-then-untouched offer. Which meant he had to ask me for my

---

[21] Insert fireworks here.

number and we had to set a "date" to meet up at the shop. But the real cake topper was when he said, "We could grab a bite to eat after." *I'll bite you.*[22] You best believe I was dying inside when he "asked me out to dinner."

We agreed to meet at 6:30 p.m., but of course I was overzealous with the whole bit and got there earlier and *had* to buy a new shirt because guys totally notice that kind of stuff. (No. No, they do not.) I was ready—ready for him to come clean to me about having a crush on me the whole semester. I mean, I knew he did. He had to have, right?

Oh gosh, that night, it was so magical—magically awkward. Now say it with me everyone: "train wreck." First of all, I made him stand outside of the shop while I bought the shoes, since all of the sudden the management was being stingy about discounts to non-family members. Then when it came time for dinner, we went to the food court. I was ahead of him in the line and when the lady asked me, "Together or separate?" I promptly spurted out, "Separate." *Ugh. You dummy.* HMG looked at me oddly like, "Okay, you psychopath." Then when we sat to eat our romantic Rubio's tacos in the oh-so ambient lighting of the food court, we sat in complete silence. Awkward. *Ask him about...umm...*

It was a disaster, an absolute disaster. To make matters even more catastrophic, I never heard from him after that day. Two days later, we took our final, and he finished way ahead of me—little did I know that this was symbolic for our future intimate relations—and left. That bastard didn't wait for me! So, I deleted his number and decided to move on with my life. (Oh, so dramatic.)

And so, my V-card pulling hopes were dashed and I would have to wear the albatross of my virginity into my second semester of college, where I met my first boyfriend, Straight Edge[23] Sissy. Straight Edge Sissy, or SES, is so-named because he was exactly that: a straight edge, whining sissy.

---

[22] I had only kissed two guys before and got so nervous for a first kiss that I actually loathed it, so biting a crush wasn't exactly on my agenda.

[23] For those of you who don't know, straight edge is a subculture of hardcore punk. They don't engage in promiscuous sex, drugs, or alcohol. Some get a little crazier and more restrictive with it...They're such rebels.

SES and I met through a mutual friend in our Philosophy of Logic class. I had seen SES pass by me in the hallway before I walked into class and, lo and behold, he sat right by my friends and me. *Huh?* Straight Edge Sissy was another one like Hot Math Guy—not particularly cute but he dressed well enough to make eighteen-year-old me swoon a bit. Besides, who was I to judge a guy? I was still fluffy from my regular therapy sessions with Ben and Jerry. Plus, I still hadn't a clue of how men actually operated.

We were introduced and sort of hit it off in an immature class clown kind of way. Straight Edge Sissy was a smart-ass, and I had a big ass, so I thought he was hysterical. We started hanging out in a group and then eventually just the two of us. It was the first time in my life that a guy took me out on real dates. In a way, SES was cute. He would plan these little dates and adventures where we would get dressed up and go out on the town like mini adults. We thought we were like the coolest and, in all truthfulness, he was a great guy to introduce me to dating.

We had been together for about four months and my hormones were raging. I wanted sex, but Straight Edge Sissy wouldn't give it to me. We had done basically everything else under the sun...Endless makeout sessions? Check. Frisky finger times? Check. Head? Check. (And it took everything in me to not bite down and then not to barf when he came...It was my first time.)

I will clarify now, I didn't want to have sex just because everyone else was doing it. I wanted it because I wanted to experience it for myself. I wanted to have sex because I somehow knew it would take our relationship to the next level. But, our journey into further relations kept getting denied, or, more specifically, I kept getting denied. *Why?*

SES had a girlfriend in high school who he'd had sex with (ugh, that bitch was always around their house, hanging out with his sister and talking shit on my fat ass even though she had a huge projector for a forehead) and he would ALWAYS compare the possibility of us having sex to the wretched humps they'd had.[24] SES didn't want to hurt me,

---

[24] Note: If any guys are reading this, know that no female ever wants to be compared to an ex...just saying.

he'd always say, but moreover, he didn't want to deal with the messiness that came with taking a girl's virginity. Whether he was talking about my emotions or my hymen was something I was never clear on.

So now you're wondering, why do I keep calling him a sissy and a pussy? Well, here's why: the one thing about SES that bothered the hell out of me was that he didn't know how to stick up for himself (or, *HELLO,* me! His girlfriend!). If someone were to say to him, "You're gay," and meant it as an insult, he would respond in the most flamboyant way possible. He used absolutely no logic in his arguments, though, ironically, we met in a Philosophy of Logic class—SES was just going for laughs. A class clown forever. Big deal, right?

Well, there soon came a time when I did care. One of his friends, whom we shall call Toe (because, well, he looked and still looks like a big toe) came over to Straight Edge Sissy's house with two others. SES and I had just gotten back from the gym, so we were eating some cereal. I had just brought the spoon to my mouth when Toe asked him, "How does it feel knowing that you're skinnier than your girlfriend?" *Ouch.* I just about died while my sweet, Straight Edge Sissy sat there. He didn't say anything! He didn't respond at all, only looked at Toe as if to say he knew but it didn't matter because he wasn't going to fight him. But it did matter. It mattered to me. I was eighteen and uncomfortable in my body as it was, plus I had been working on eating healthier and working out again, and although my progress had been slow and subtle, I had lost some weight. I was mortified.

But, oh no, Toe didn't stop there. He continued with the low blows. I can't reiterate it to you enough—guys talk. They're little secretive gossiping fiends!

"So, Dax, how's the sex life going?" Toe hissed.

How about my knee in your balls? I stared.

"Because I heard that SES won't have sex with you," he stabbed.

You do know that you look like a toe, right? I was fuming.

Still nothing out of Straight Edge Sissy and I'd had enough. SES wasn't doing anything about Toe, and Toe didn't know when to shut the fuck up.

"Ah, you're right, he won't have sex with me, and, *oh god,* have I been begging him. But, wait, now that I'm thinking about it, how's your girlfriend doing, Toe?" All eyes were on us. Toe stood there silent, glaring back at me. "Oh what's that you say…you don't have a girlfriend?" I asked, rubbing salt in his wound. "Ah, so that means you don't have sex? Okay, just checking." *Check and mate.*

You could see it in Toe's beady eyes—he hated me. I didn't care. After a couple beats of silence had been interrupted by the laughter of their other two friends, Toe's only retort was, "Hardy har har. Good one, Dax." I knew that Tweedledee and Tweedledumb cracking up at Toe's expense was the one thing he cared about. All he wanted to do was look cool when everyone knew that his fat-phalanges-ass didn't have a chance of getting with a girl. So, I left the room while SES and Toe just stood there in the perilous silence left hanging in my wake. *Fuck them.*

It was toward the end of the second semester, and SES and I had been dating for the whole of it. I wanted to break up with him. I was sick of his stupid jokes, his wretched music (which was also a joke) and his god-awful friends who made our relationship the butt of every joke. Of everything, SES's jokes were the worst. They were repetitive and childish and always passive aggressive. Or perhaps I was just angry and full of pent-up sexual frustration. Maybe that was what was really bothering me, I was eighteen and I thought I knew what I wanted. I naively thought sex would be simple.

My breaking point came in the form of a gorgeous guy in my Spanish 3 class. Because what more incentive does a girl need to break up with her boyfriend who is slowly and most certainly becoming the bane of her existence than a hottie who knows how to roll his R's, if you're catching my drift.

The Spanish class guy was kind of a pompous dick, but that was only a minor obstacle since he was so *guapo.* We had worked on an entire project together for two weeks in class, but Guapo would never talk to me. If he did, it was always in this passive manner about the project and he'd never make eye contact. *This is driving me nuts.* Well, a couple of classes after our project wrapped up, Guapo came up to me and said, "Hey, you know my roommate."

"Who's your roommate?" I managed to spurt out through my flabbergasted state.

"Oh, it's [Hot Math Guy]." Guapo answered.

"Yeah, he was in my math class last semester."

"Rad, he's mentioned you a few times." Guapo nodded in his cool surfer way, swaying his whole body like a giant wave.

Oh my god…HMG talks about me?

"You should come kick it with us at our place and we can all go out," Guapo offered. He must have seen the shock on my face and reassured me by repeating his invite.

It's okay if you think I'm a horrible person now. For weeks (yes, even before Guapo told me to "kick it" with him and HMG), I had been plotting how I would break up with SES. I didn't know how to do that shit! I had never done that before. I confided in our friend who had introduced us and his response was, "I told you he was annoying." *Oops, must've missed that memo.* Although he didn't tell me how to break up with SES, he did tell me that I should probably start hanging out with SES less. So, I took his advice and started making myself unavailable to Straight Edge Sissy. Poor guy, I could tell he was freaking out and getting suspicious.

We still hung out a couple of times a week, but I made sure to not always be available and to definitely not always have my phone on me. I swear I wasn't using this as a ploy to get him to have sex with me, but something must have clicked in his peanut brain because one night, he finally offered in the midst of a heavy make out sesh: "Should I put a condom on?" *Sissy say what?*

I stopped my lips dead in their slobber tracks. The way he said it. It was so unattractive and unsure. I was turned off by his squeaky-voiced question. *Is this fool for real?* All of the sudden it had come time for me to put my money where my mouth was. The thing that I had been begging to do for at least a month and now and I was debilitatingly nervous because of the way he said it? All I wanted was for a man to take charge and show me how it's done—you know, show me the ropes. *Uhh what am I supposed to do?*

The lights were off, and the room was as dark as a birth canal. SES rolled over toward his dresser, fumbling through his top drawer and then, I heard it…the crinkling of a condom wrapper. My stomach sunk. *Don't you dare back out. This is what you want. Maybe this will change the way you feel about him.* SES rolled back over to face me. He ripped open the wrapper and ruined the pep talk I had been giving myself when he squeaked, "You put it on."

Nope. "No. You're the guy. You put it on."

So after some hesitation (on his part—I was going to make myself do it), SES put the condom on himself and my engines went from revved and ready to cold and disinterested. At this point, any momentum we had created to flow into sex had fizzled, and I was totally unprepared for this horrid shit of a first time.

"Okay, get on top of me," SES whined.

"Um, okay?" *SES, you're an idiot and I don't want to do this anymore.* I got on top of him anyway.

"Now put it in."

That moron was seriously just laying on his back, barking sissy orders but too scared to touch me. I didn't want to pop my *OWN* cherry; I wanted a *MAN* to pop it for me (with my consent of course). Regardless, I grabbed his only manly trait and tried to sit on it but quickly realized that he was gross and not what I wanted. *Nope.* I wasn't about to let this happen.

Right about now, you might be wondering how a drama queen like me gets out of such a tangled experience. "Oooh, no…Forget it," I moaned as I thudded on top of him, collapsing down and rolling off. "You've had sex before. You should be on top," I said reminding him of his experience.

No comment from the peanut gallery.

That night I made up my mind, I would break up with him that week. I had already made plans to hang out with my new "friends" the following week since the semester had ended; showing up as a radiantly single woman sounded like the way to go.

The next day, SES texted me and wanted to grab lunch, but I told him I couldn't. I said I had to get ready for work (which wasn't a complete lie). I could hear the disappointment in his voice through the sad words he punched out in his response text, but I had to stick to my guns otherwise I would be a miserable woman. He then promptly prophesied that I was going to break up with him. (Oops. He must've read the apology poem I'd written on my blog and probably figured out that it was to him. My bad.) "Just do it," he texted me. *Stop. I want to do this in person.* This is when he got super annoying and childish and started blowing up my phone with a repeating snow flurry of "just do it." *Okay, Nike, settle down.*

I did what I thought to be the responsible adult thing: I called him. He continued to provoke me over the phone, attempting to get me to break up with him over the phone. Well, I took the bait, "[SES] I can't do this anymore."

"Fine."

"I'm sorry, I just need to be alone." *Away from your immature jokes.*

"I knew you were going to break up with me," he whined into the phone.

"I'm sorry." I said and I meant it. I truly was sorry.

"Why?"

Because you're annoying as all hell and I don't think a girl will ever take you seriously. "I'm just sorry," I sang into the receiver through tears.

"Whatever," he spat. I could tell he was fighting back tears. "Are we done with this?"

"Yeah, bye." *Click. Woohoo! We're done!*

I felt bad for ending things with Straight Edge Sissy. Not because I thought we would work things out but because he was so annoying, I didn't think he could ever get another girlfriend or really understand how immature he was himself. (I was wrong. He did get another girlfriend. Good for him and good luck to her.) I was giving myself high props, though, for successfully and (somewhat) maturely tackling my first non-high-school breakup.

Five days later, SES called me as I was getting ready to meet up with Hot Math Guy and Guapo. He sounded like a wreck. "I just need to see you and talk to you in person."

Dipshit, that's why I wanted to do this in person the first time. "I'm getting ready to go out with my friends," I said in an attempt to alleviate myself from this unexpected nuisance.

"I need to talk to you." He sounded desperate.

I thought we were done! "Fine, I'll be by in thirty."

"Okay, see you soon," he bellyached.

I wanted to make it as quick as possible. I had a hot non-date to get to and, to be completely honest, I was afraid that I was going to cry if things took an emotional route.[25]

I pulled up to his house, and in no more than two seconds, SES was out the door. (That's how I like my men to be, on their toes.) We decided to take a walk around the neighborhood to "talk about it." I knew that the walk was about ten minutes since we had walked it infinite times before with his dogs, so I eased into the "talk" knowing that it would all be over in six hundred seconds. Plus, knowing I was about to meet up with Guapo and HMG brightened up the light at the end of my tunnel. Nothing could bring me down.

To spare you the boredom of yet another pointless conversation with Straight Edge Sissy, I explained to him why I made my decision to end things—which is to say, I lied. I embellished my need to focus on school, "so I can transfer out of that hell hole," and waxed poetic about how I couldn't afford anymore distractions. Now, this was maybe a little bit of an exaggeration but I couldn't exactly tell him that he was annoying the shit out of me.

However genuine I sounded, SES had decided to be as immature as humanly possible and argued with me about everything. I would not give in; I had no desire to engage in his petty ways. Then, in a moment that perfectly illustrated him and our relationship, an opossum ran out of the bushes and across our path. SES screamed and jumped behind *me*, using my body as a shield to block himself from a harmless marsupial. That more than assured me that I had made the right decision to breakup with him. SES was embarrassed, and I was irritated, and there wasn't a doubt in my mind that that was the end. It was over.

---

[25] I'm just like my mother.

I left SES in the dust (I should have pushed him into the bushes) as I jammed over to Guapo and HMG's. That night we went out to one of the local bars where one of their friend's bands was playing.[26] We all got a nice buzz going. It was Guapo, HMG, their other roommate, and me, and I was having the time of my life. I was eighteen, and everyone else was twenty-four or older. I thought I was so cool!

The band's set ended and the bar was doing last call. The three of us left—Guapo, HMG and I since their other roommate wanted to continue the party at the bar down the road. We walked through the streets joking around, teasing each other and reminiscing over stories from our earlier days. I can still picture us walking down the darkened winding road to their house, filling the sleeping streets with laughter and bliss. It had been awhile since I had felt so welcomed by a group of people and I was swallowing every second of it. When we made it back to the house, all three of us crashed on their huge couch. The next morning, I woke up, put my shoes on and left.

From only one night, I knew that I loved spending time with them. They were all cool and laid back, artsy-types. That group of people made me feel like an adult instead of some dumb lost teenager struggling to find herself. It was like they understood the sadness that I had locked myself into for so many years, like they could see that there was a real person deep inside, ready to face the world. They weren't blinded by my tough girl façade. Somehow, they saw past it. I was an adult to them, regardless of my age or the struggles I had struggled, and they all seemed to genuinely care about me.

A few hours later, Guapo texted me, asking where I had gone and if I wanted to go out with them later that week. Of course, I answered yes, any attention-starved eighteen-year-old girl would. Then HMG texted me, wanting to make sure I had gotten home safely and asking me exactly what Guapo had already asked. I had found my people.

A few days later, I showed up at their place dressed and ready to go. The house was a mess with people. Bodies sprawled across the living

---

[26] Did I mention I had a fake ID from a girl in my French class that totally worked/ the bar didn't actually check my ID. Shame on them!

room floor and the kitchen bubbled over with persons engaged in a high stakes beer pong game. *Whoa, this is fun!* Hot Math Guy came charging at me from the kitchen, leaving his game of beer pong to sweep me up in a hearty hug. I was probably blushing. Ah fuck it, I was blushing. "Whoa, fella!" I awkwardly squealed, patting his back.

"Haha, can I get you a drink?" my hospitable host asked.

"Sure," I grinned.

"What'll you be having?"

Just then, some voices from the kitchen taunted, "Hey, you're gonna lose, bro."

HMG didn't seem to care, "Ah, I already spanked you guys...so what can I get you?"

"Um, how about whatever you're having?"

"Rum and coke it is."

I smirked. He squeezed my arm as he darted back to the kitchen to prepare our drinks. My head was spinning with his touch and the anticipation of a stiff drink. But suddenly my boy-drunken haze was broken.

"Hey Dax!"

"Hi [Guapo]..."

"Where's your drink?"

"Oh, [HMG] is making it."

"Rad...cheers then."

I fist-pumped his beer can as Hot Math Guy returned with drinks in hand. I sipped on my drink while the rest of the house drank itself dry. The time had come—bars, baby!

We didn't stay out late, in fact, HMG and I, along with his roommate and his girlfriend left earlier than everyone else. When we got back to the house, it was a mess of silence. Empty bottles and cans ornamented the kitchen and living room while the fridge sulked with vacancy. Not a single thing was left to eat or drink.

Seeing as we were all a little buzzed, the roommate's girlfriend suggested that someone go to the liquor store up the street since she was "too drunk to see straight." (Okay, so some of us were drunker than others.) HMG volunteered himself and asked me to go with him. I agreed and off we went on to another adventure.

The air was damp and the marine layer thick, but we were beaming with a new romance. As we walked side by side up the hill to the liquor store, HMG grabbed my hand. I jumped a little as my heart skipped a beat or two. He had startled me; I had not expected him to hold my hand. Naively, I had thought we were only going to be friends and that I was the only one with the forbidden feelings for him. WRONG! He held my hand all the way up the hill, through the liquor store and back down, only letting go to open the front door to his house.

By the time we got back, Guapo had come home and passed out on the couch with the T.V. blasting while the other roommate and his girlfriend had knocked out in their room. We put the sugar and salt loaded munchies away and sat on the other end of the couch. A few minutes passed by in silence as we blankly stared at the skate video playing on the T.V. Then HMG got up: "I'm going to watch a movie in my room."

"Oh, okay, I'll just crash here if that's okay?"

He nodded his head and walked the ten feet to his room then did an abrupt about-face, "You don't have to watch this. You can watch a movie with me."

Oh. I was so naive; I had no idea what HMG was suggesting. I didn't know he wanted to "watch" a movie with me and it certainly did not cross my mind that "watching" a movie really meant not watching a movie.

He gently grabbed my hand as he led me to his room. "Sorry, my room is kind of a mess. What do you want to watch?"

We sat on his bed with our backs to the wall and flipped through his Netflix[27] before settling on some *Hey Arnold* cartoons. (Raise your hand if you used to watch *Hey Arnold*…now raise your hand if you lost your virginity to *Hey Arnold*.) It started off innocently enough; there wasn't any touching or petting, just a whole lot of awkward tension.

---

[27] Am I patient zero for Netflix and Chill?

We watched an episode and started another one when I responded to something Helga[28] said. "Haha, what?" HMG asked me.

I turned to him to repeat myself, "I said—" Only he met my words with a kiss. *Oh my god, oh my god, oh my god. Hot Math Guy kissed me!* I broke away to look him in the eyes, giggling, and then he grabbed me tighter and kissed me again. Kissing slowly turned into us making out which transcended me into the heavenly haze of my own fantasies. *What happens now? Will we live here or move somewhere else? What will our wedding be like? Are we going to be like the trendiest couple ever? I wonder how many kids he wants? Will our kids skate too?*

HMG was older and experienced, and I was young and, frankly, dumb. All of my older girlfriends at work had warned me of how attached they had gotten to their "first," and I had waved them off like the twats that they were, continuing my long awaited make out session. What seemed like forever went by when HMG finally took his hand behind my head and laid me down. It was like a well-choreographed dance and he knew all of the steps while I hadn't a clue which was my left and which way was my right. Making out turned in to petting, which turned to the slow stripping down of clothes. He knew exactly what he was doing, and I was gleefully allowing him to lead the way.

There I was, back to the bed and saggy breasts to the sky. Nothing but a thin thong and striped briefs kept us apart. "Hold on," HMG said before he walked to his closet and pulled out a little box. Returning to the bed with a condom in one hand, he hooked his finger to the side of my underwear as he gracefully pulled them down, then yanked his own down without the same care. He laid back beside me as he rolled the condom on. *Yes. I'm going to do this.*

With his back to the bed, he turned toward me and started kissing and touching me again. This was the way that I wanted to lose my blasphemous virginity. He rolled over on top of me, framing my face with his hands, not once breaking the kiss. I could feel him; he was ready and I was more than ready. He broke the kiss and locked eyes with me. Right before he put it in, I put my hand to his chest,

---

[28] Helga is the mean blonde in *Hey Arnold*, obviously she and I have a lot in common.

"Wait...I'm a virgin."

Doh! He paused for a second and searched my eyes while his eyes darted back and forth in a mix fear and confusion.

Probably not the sexiest thing to say to someone that was about to deflower me, but HMG didn't seem to care (I mean he did, but he didn't). Our sinning carried on unhitched with some of us being more active participants than others.[29] It didn't seem to bother him and it wasn't like it was the last time we "did it."

I will say that the girls at work were right and I did get excruciatingly attached to HMG (but don't we always get attached with sex?). Your first is and will always be the one that sticks with you—but let's be honest, they all stick with you.

Hot Math Guy was sweet and patient with me, but there is only so much naivety a man can take. Our sex-filled relationship lasted about a month after we threw down, and I can assure you I wanted to spend every waking moment with him. I tried my hardest to not always inquire his whereabouts and doings, and I think I did kind of okay playing the whole thing aloof, but when the time came that HMG began to distance himself from me, I could feel the crazy spewing out of my brain. *C'est la vie.* You live and you learn, and boy did I learn a lot. Sex is a power monger, and she makes a bitch feel thirsty!

Things ended with Hot Math Guy, and I was devastated but didn't blame him for it at all. I knew that he needed a woman and not some girl who was trying to be a woman. I accepted our fate and moved on (kind of, I stalked his social media a lot). I started to work more since it was summer and decided to try out for our school soccer team to distract myself and as a means to ditch the last bit of depression that I had been fighting through since high school, after I had torn my ACL. So, I was completely healed up and ready for a new chapter in my life Enter *El Colombiano.*

---

[29] I dead-fished him...I was inexperienced, what did you expect?

VIVA LA HEARTBREAK PART 1

Latin men like 'em husky.

I was eighteen, a week away from my nineteenth birthday. Life was slowly fitting back together. Eighteen had been a hard year—leaving the cruelty of high school, being rejected by every university under the sun, and losing everyone that I had called a friend. The transition from seventeen to eighteen was daunting, and I loathed myself and everyone else. I was not my favorite person, and I can guarantee that I definitely would not have been yours. But what more could you expect from a juvenile who felt like her world was ending? So, as my eighteenth year came to a close, I warmly welcomed my nineteenth "guaranteed to be better than this shit" year with flabby open arms.[30]

During this time, I worked for a big, international, swoosh-for-a-logo company. That summer we were busy. They were expanding the boutique section of the company, the money was crap, and the bonuses were nonexistent, but it was much better than staying stuck in my head at home, mourning the loss of my virginity-slayer.

It was just another hapless day, and so god-awful hot outside that I had to wear shorts—I hate wearing shorts. The only clean shirt I had was this ugly, ill-fitting charcoal pink tank top and my hair was probably dirty since I was in the middle of my "I don't wash my hair because I think I'm so hip" phase. Needless to say, I was in a shit mood, and the last thing I wanted to do was work. Too bad for me, the store was BUSY! The swoosh-logo brand had just released a new collector's

---

[30] Yes, I was still working off that ice cream therapy fat.

shoe, which meant we barely had time to take a breath between phone calls and in-store customers.

I was confined to the chokehold of an office in the back of the store, taking phone orders and keeping an eye on the cameras, when in he walked—tall, lean, creamy coffee-colored skin, and perfectly tousled bed head. (Yes, I am creepy enough to notice all of this from a tiny security camera screen). This guy's look screamed out "foreign babe!!!" You better believe I left that stuffy office to catch a breath of fresh air.

Hellos were exchanged, hands were shaken, names were given, and paths were parted. I had discovered that he played for the Colombian men's national water polo team and, apart from that, I hadn't gotten much more in that minuscule introduction. Nonetheless, I was on a high. My mind was set on overdrive. He was Colombian, and my mom's family is Colombian. *Whoa.* I've always said that my white side is my bad side and that I liked the Colombian half much more. The romantic possibilities of having similar Colombian lineages were so alluring to me. This *Colombiano* grew up eating rice, beans, and *arepas*, and I grew up eating rice, beans, and *arepas*. He was like a unicorn to me, and I wanted him.

Half past noon struck and I was sent on my merry way. I had thirty ephemeral minutes to stuff my face before I had to return to the glory of the store. I couldn't stop thinking about him. I wished I had given him my phone number or at least made plans to watch his water polo match. *Ugh, I'm such a dunce!!! I am so weird! Why do I act shy?!* As I walked to Starbucks, I was blinded by the different scenarios I played out in my head—there were so many other things I should have said to him. I was so absorbed in my thoughts that I walked right past the magical *Colombiano*, who was seated just outside the doors of Starbucks. Oblivious was I.

I grabbed my cellulite-adding lunch and zoomed out the door with plans to return to the wretched, sunless office in the back of the store, and then I saw him, from the corner of my right eye as I shot past him. There he was, sitting smugly under the shade of an oversized umbrella. So what did I do? I'll tell you what I should have done—I should have asked to sit with him since we had made eye contact. I should have plopped my ass right next to him and eaten my lunch there. But instead, being my blundering, half-wit, almost-nineteen-year-old self, I consciously walked by him yet again, while gracelessly avoiding eye contact. I sat my pasty white *derrière* on an incredibly uncomfortable cement planter, just a little ways down from where he sat. Then, to make myself all the more undesirable, I whipped out my phone and called my mother…I didn't want to look like I didn't have anything important going on and being on your phone always makes you look important (…and insecure).

Our eyes kept catching, but I was so uncomfortably excited by El Colombiano that I would dart mine away as soon as they met. He was beautiful and he looked like he had the world figured out, and I wanted to be in that world. I was dumbfounded by him but you couldn't tell because I am always so collected—taking huge bites of my dried-out turkey sandwich, watching as the crumbs cascaded from my gaping hole of a mouth as I tried to string together comprehensive words over the phone to my mom. *Now stop eating, grab your drink and take a sip. Hold your coffee up. Now laugh because you're so cool. Okay, okay, okay. Stop. Is he looking? Oh, god.*

This amateurish dance continued for about fifteen minutes until I had a stroke of genius and decided to throw my lunch away, not in the trash can located a few yards away from me but the one situated just behind his seat. So, up I popped, gallivanting toward the mystery that sat ahead of me. Once again, I played dumb and blind as I threw away my trash. My pudgy stomach still growling, protesting with hunger, but I needed the excuse to rear myself in his direction. The reality is that I needed no explanation. He knew I wanted to talk to him, and I knew he wanted to talk to me…the chubby white blonde girl and Latino man go hand-in-hand.

We once again engaged in a brief and meaningless conversation, yet this time information was exchanged, and hope was cultivated. He was magic, and I was riding high for the rest of the day…until I returned home and realized that idiotically, I hadn't saved his information into my crap Blackberry phone. Devastation has never been so devastating. I almost cried. Shit, I think I did cry.

The thought ran rampant through my mind for a couple of days. *How could I not save that? How could I be so stupid?* Those pestering thoughts were put to a halting stop three days later when a new Facebook friend request came in…ACCEPT! He had found me; Colombiano had actually gone through all of the girls on Facebook with my name and found me! I don't know how the hell he did, but he did it.

I screamed, "Mom! He found me! This is the Colombian guy."

"That's great, honey," she placated me.

"Oh my god, he's such a babe! Look…look…look."

"Hold on! Do you want your lunch or not?" (Sometimes she's unnecessarily aggressive.)

I started stalking through his pictures while I waited for my Mommy Dearest to come see this hunk of a man I had found for myself. *There he is with his family, his dog, ahhh, his grandma. Wow, there he is under a waterfall looking so sexy in Calvin Klein's. Whoa, there he is in some tight leather pants…Hold up—here's a link to YouTube? What?! What?! I think I'm going to die. He's a model…Uhhhh he's riding a motorcycle in skintight leather pants and a leather jacket. Grrrrr, look at those abs. Hot damn, Papi.*

I was so enveloped by his glamour that I failed to notice the little red notification above my messages. Colombiano had messaged me, inviting me to his water polo game that Thursday at the prep school just fifteen minutes away from my house.

We shot messages back and forth for an hour or so. Talking about everything and nothing. His English was awful, and my Spanish was worse. Thank goodness for my mom and her willingness to translate for me. Eventually, we said goodbye when he had to leave for training, knowing that we would see each other in a few days or so. He said goodbye and probably filled his head with water polo, I said goodbye and filled my head with him. He was just so hot. I couldn't wrap my recently de-virginized head around the fact that he was interested in me!

Sunday, Monday, Tuesday, and Wednesday had all come and gone, and Thursday had finally arrived. Colombiano and I had talked nearly all day, every day. The only time we weren't talking was when he had to go to training or when I was at work or soccer practice (but I would always sneak away to message him back). I was enamored by his mispronunciations, misspellings, and misunderstandings. Everything he did was adorable to me, and we had only been talking through Facebook Messenger (those were the days before international messaging apps WhatsApp and Viber, for all you young'uns out there).

That Thursday, I had asked my fourteen-year-old sister to accompany me to beautiful Colombiano's water polo game. There we were, two boy-crazed sisters, the only (half) white girls rooting for an all-Colombian men's water polo team. *Wait, which one is he?*

He was a vision, caramel-colored skin, chiseled abs and a smile for days. My sister and I manically giggled when I pointed him out, and she realized that he had been looking over at us in between shots on goal during their warmup (he was the goalie). Then we realized that the whole water polo team was staring at us...See I told you guys talk! I felt like the queen of the world sitting atop of those bleachers looking down at nearly naked men, knowing that they kept looking up to us. (Talk about empowerment of women.)

The game ended and we all congregated in the corner of the pool area. Colombiano introduced us to everyone, but I had a tough time remembering all of their names since they were all mostly naked and some of them were even changing out of their speedos in front of us. *Hi, I'm Dong...I mean Dax. God, thank you for not making me a boy, then I'd never be able to hide how I felt.*

We all simmered around the pool for thirty minutes or so, and then their coach called us back to reality when he dictated to the men that it was time to return to their hotel for dinner. *Uhh, excuse me, I am trying to be won over by this model of a man!*

"Hey, Daxie." I hate "Daxie," but if that's what he wanted to call me, then I would take it.

"Yeah?"

"Maybe you'n Candle can dinner wit us." Candle is not my sister's name but apparently her real name is difficult to say with an accent.

I looked to Candle, and she gave me a smirk that said, "Hell yeah."

"Yes, but I have to ask my mom first."

"Hey, Daxie, *en español*..." (Hey, Daxie, in Spanish.)

"*Primero, tengo que preguntar mi mamá.*" (First, I have to ask my mom.)

"*Ay, claro que sí.*" (Oh, of course.)

I wanted to go hang out with them so badly. In hindsight, this definitely sounded sketchy, but I assure you that we were completely safe and I would've never subjected myself and *especially* not my sister, to any danger.

"Can you send me your address?"

"Eh?" (White girl say what?)

"*¿Puedes enviarme tu dirección?*" (Can you send me your address?)

"*Claro, cuando regresamos al hotel, te enviaré la dirección.*" (Of course, when we return to the hotel, I will send you our address.)

"*Perfecto! Nos vemos. Ciao.*" (Perfect, see you soon. Bye...*I love you.*)

Giddy, I was giddy. My whole body was set aflame. My eyes twinkling, my heart fluttering, and my skin tingling. Colombiano was amazing and I wanted him. I needed him.

My sister and I walked back to my unreliable, 1993 Honda Civic, watching as the perfectly chiseled men piled into two white vans.[31] Smiling and waving them off, our faces said it all and nothing could stop that feeling. Hunching into our car and buckling our seat belts, my fingers strummed a series of numbers onto my phone's keyboard. *Ring....ring...ring...*I passed my phone off to my sister. She knew what to do when our mother answered the other end of that call. Candle knew that she had to dazzle our mother with every romantic detail in order for us to be allowed to meet my future soulmate at his hotel. She understood just how important this phone call was to me...to my future...I mean, to my and Colombiano's future.

My mother answered and Candle sounded sweeter than ever. They carried on their conversation for a minute or two. My baby sister filled my office-entrapped mother in on every detail, every glance glanced, every smirk smirked, and every breath breathed. I sat back in my overused car and listened, reminiscing on every second of that game. Candle shot me a glance that could only mean one thing: my mother

---

[31] Well, that sounds creepy.

wanted to talk to me. Did my dreams stand a chance? *Is there hope for me to see Colombiano again tonight?*

My mother and I spoke for a blip of a second, in which she asked me exactly what she had already asked my sister. I answered accordingly, and, of course flamboyantly detailed every bit of it the way a dumb, love-struck teenager would. Mama was eating it up. She was almost taunting me by questioning me for more info. She wanted no detail to be spared (which is why I am a psycho with details). She chuckled a few chuckles, ahhed a plethora of ahhs and agreed to let us go meet up with the Colombiano and his team.[32]

So there we were, two teenage girls jumping out of our skins with anticipation, waiting for the promised Facebook message to confirm our meeting place. The seconds were ticking by into minutes and the minutes felt like hours. *I can't take it anymore!* I remembered Colombiano mentioning his hotel and, since I was always buzzing around in my overheating '93 Civic, I knew exactly where it was (even though it was like four cities away). So as a collective union of two, my sister and I decided that it would be best if we headed that way since it was so "far." Engine revving (and probably smoking a bit) and Dashboard Confessional blasting through my blown-out speakers, we headed toward the far kingdom that held my handsome prince captive.

Somewhere between here and there, we realized that it may have been a tad creepy (just a tad) if we just showed up out of the blue. Okay, fine! *WE* didn't realize, Candle called me out on it, "Did he send you the address yet?" she asked smugly.

"I don't know. Check my Facebook," I replied without even questioning my actions.

She grabbed my phone from the cupholder and opened up my Facebook messenger. Nothing. "He hasn't sent you anything. How do you know where you're going?"

"I just do."

---

[32] I know what you're thinking but she didn't just "let us go." We had to give her the address and check in with her periodically *and* we had an early curfew. My mother is a woman who tells us to choose for ourselves based on our own judgments and, damn it, I chose for myself!

"Dax, you can't do that?"

"Do what? I know where I am going," I reassured her of my navigational skills.

"Yeah, but he hasn't sent you a message yet."

"But he had mentioned his hotel already, and I know where it is."

"Well, that's creepy."

"Oh." I moaned as reality hit me.

"Yeah, *oh*. We should stop," Candle suggested.

"Yeah, we'll probably be hungry soon."

"Okay, where are we going to stop?"

"There's a Starbucks just off the next exit"

So we took a detour from the kingdom that lay far, far away to occupy ourselves with burnt coffee and plastic pastries. Fortunately, Candle and I sat for no more than ten minutes when suddenly the backlight of my Blackberry Pearl zinged to life with a Facebook message from my beloved.

We were thrilled, bordering on hysterical, as we galloped back to our heinous and outdated chariot of a car. Maddened was I as I wove in and out of slowing traffic. Singing we were and relieved was Candle when my car finally halted to a stop at their hotel. The car parked, our seat belts unbuckled, and our doors swung open. There he was, Colombiano, waiting atop the third story of his dingy castle-of-a-motel. Our doors slammed shut, echoing through the barren weed-ridden parking lot, coaxing Colombiano out of his high tower and down to us.

He met us with a big hug and invited us up to their room. I was wracked with nerves, but Candle seemed unfazed (she had nothing at stake, whereas I had the heart of my beloved hanging in front of my hungry soul). We walked up the two flights of stairs to their apartment-sized hotel room on the third floor. The room was a mess with drying speedos hung throughout and clothes and bodies sprawling across floors and beds. The guys cleared a space on the couch for Candle and me to sit, then they gathered around us.

The room filled with laughter and loud voices as we all told stories of our homes. Each one of us wanted to practice the foreign language of the other. Many of our stories were broken up into a mix of English and Spanish depending on who didn't understand the language of the story. It was magic. The spacious room seemed to shrink in size as more bodies piled in front of the storyteller and wonderment of the aliens that sat before them.

Hours passed like seconds and the time had come for us to return to our home in a land far, far away. Candle and I said goodbye to the welcoming water polo team and were accompanied out by Colombiano and one of his teammates. They walked us to our car, not missing a beat in the conversation, then they opened our doors and hugged us goodbye. Colombiano held on to me just a tad longer and a tad tighter, while I melted into his body, praying that he wouldn't let go. But, alas, our hug was broken by the taunting of his teammate screaming at us to kiss and, since I was so new to this whole dating guys thing (yes, even after losing my virginity), I broke away and said goodnight.

We floated home in my ghettofied lemon of a car in complete silence. Both Candle and I grinning ear to ear, each of us blissfully caught up in our newly made memories. *Brrrrrrringgggg.* My phone lit up the interior of my tiny car. It was Colombiano. Like my phone, my mind lit up with the possibilities of what he had said in the message. I made myself wait until we were inside of our home and I was in my bed to read his message.

While tucking[33] into bed and swaddling my mind with thoughts of Colombiano, I opened his message. He had thanked my sister and me for entertaining them and driving to see him. He then asked me if I would like to go out with him for ice cream after his game in a couple of days…*Uh, duh, I want to go out with you.* I promptly responded while silencing my urge to scream out loud. *He asked me on a date! Oh my gosh, I wonder where we will go? What should I wear? What kind of ice cream will he order? What kind should I order? Should I get a small? Woohoo! I should tell my mom.*

---

[33] Don't Google "tucking," it will pop up with how to tuck yourself as a man to become a woman…unless you were sincerely curious. I was just looking for a synonym.

So I screamed from my bedroom across the short hall to my mother's room, "Hey, Mom!" No answer, so I continued, "Mom!" Still no answer, and I wasn't about to get out of bed so I tried once more, "Hey, Mom! Mommmmmmm!"

"What DAX?!" she shouted back.

"Guess what?"

"What," she stated. There was no curiousness in her voice to make it into a question.

"He just asked me out on a date after his next game," I jumbled out.

"Wow that's great, honey."[34]

"I know! I'm so excited!!! What do you think I should wear?"

"Goodnight, Dax."

Obviously, she wasn't into my outfit conundrum, but I couldn't sleep now. Colombiano was blowing up my phone with messages, and I was blowing up my head with fantasies of him (not sexual ones, you pervs!). My cellphone illuminated my face until the wee hours of the morning when he eventually said goodnight. My head was swirling with his *palabras*,[35] and my heart was fluttering with the anticipation of our date. I finally closed my eyes and drifted off to sleep.

The days leading up to our date ticked away before I knew it. I met Colombiano at his hotel. I had to pick him up since he didn't have a car and he didn't know his way around. He wanted to go back to the place we had met: a huge outdoor mall that he was infatuated with since they don't really have anything like that in Colombia. We arrived later in the evening and, *ugh*, all of the stores were closing, so we only had time to get ice cream.

We grabbed our dessert and headed over to the carousel just down the way. The night was warm, and the mall was still crowded with the sun-kissed bodies of a southern California summer. Colombiano and I took a seat on the metal bench facing the carousel. I was so jittery with nerves that I was shaking, and it was taking everything in me to keep

---

[34] Dully note the sarcasm in her tone…so rude.

[35] That's español for words!

my teeth from chattering. I didn't want him to think I was weird. (God forbid someone find out I'm weird.)

I could barely eat my ice cream I was so riddled with nerves. I was petrified that my Spanish wouldn't be good enough to communicate with him. I was absolutely terrified that he would kiss me. *What if I'm not good at kissing? What if he doesn't like the way I kiss? What if I am so bad that he never talks to me again?*

Throughout our shared time on the bench, I fidgeted my way through moments of silence, but luckily for me, those were few and far apart even with our occasional language barrier.

Our minutes together on that cold metal bench filled with stories of our families and friends. Everything about Colombiano was sincere. And then suddenly, I felt the urge to ask him if he had a girlfriend back home. I don't know why it clicked in my brain that I should ask him such a question. He looked at me with a mouthful of ice cream and unraveled this story of how he used to have a girlfriend, but she had moved to Indonesia to study art, so they had mutually decided to break up because of the distance. (Clue Number One: distance. I should've known then.)

So he was single. I remember feeling my face warm with the goofiest of smiles thinking to myself how lucky I was. Colombiano finished his story and then looked to me to continue about myself—Was I single? I answered him, sparing him the details of my virginity slayer and going on about how I wasn't dating anyone because I wanted to focus on school and soccer. He smiled and said in his accented, broken English, "Good for me."

Sometime around ten o'clock we wrapped up our conversation and headed back to the car since Colombiano's coach had given him a curfew. I played DJ along with my role of chauffeur. I played him the few cool Spanish songs I knew. A sea of headlights raced by us as we coasted along the 5 freeway in a haze of lyrics. He reached across the center console to rest his hand on my leg. I broke my concentration from the darkened road to meet his smiling eyes. I knew then that Colombiano was going to kiss me soon and I knew then that I wasn't scared anymore of kissing this gorgeous man I had seemingly just met.

Like days before, I pulled into the same parking space that Candle and I had parked the first time. Only this time, I wasn't with my sister. I was next to the guy I had dreamt about since the moment I had met him. Just like he had done only minutes before, Colombiano reached across the center console. Only this time he grabbed my face and met my lips with a kiss. That was it. That was the moment I died and went to heaven. And like some nights before, I drove home in love-besotted bliss.

Colombiano's time in the States was coming to an end. We'd only known each other for about a week or so, but to me, that was time enough to think that I knew that he was "the one." He was smart, handsome, close to his family, and creative. It didn't worry me that I "barely" knew him, I figured we had a lifetime to know each other (I mean isn't that part of the romance?). This man was everything I was looking for in a soulmate. I didn't care if I had to move to Medellin or if he wanted to move here; we had a LIFETIME to travel and learn and love. Yes, I know, my definition of love was shallow—but Colombiano fit my criteria so perfectly that I thought myself stupid to let him just slip by.

My beloved had but one night left in the ole U.S. of A., and we had arranged to say our goodbyes later that evening since he had a team activity for most of the afternoon and I had a dinner date with my new gay best friend, Julio, from my French class. Julio had been infatuated with my Colombian Adonis since I had shown him his pictures. (I thought Julio was going to pass out when he saw the Calvin Klein waterfall pictures.)

In fact, most of that night with Julio consisted of him preparing me to have sex with my Colombiano. He was making me so nervous! All I could do was keep saying, "No, no, no." From the minute Julio climbed in my car, throughout our dinner, and for the duration of our nightcap back at his house, my answer was "No." And Julio would say in response, "Yes, betch."

I meant my "no's" though. I just wasn't ready to have sex with this man that was to be forever mine. (Yes, I am deranged.) I figured I had my entire life with Colombiano to build toward the explosive, mind-blowing sex that we'd surely have.[36] "Besides," I added, "I know how attached I'll get once we do it." But Julio was insistent, and he told me he wanted to live out his Latino model fantasy through me.

"Sooo, basically you are telling me to channel you while I'm having sex with Colombiano?" I asked incredulously.

"YES." Julio was relentless.

Finally (and thankfully) it was time for me to go meet my beloved for one last time before he flew away. Little did I know that while I ran to the bathroom, Julio mischievously placed two condoms in my purse...one ribbed and one strawberry flavored (subliminal messaging?). Cluelessly, I grabbed my bag and kissed him goodbye. "I left you a little surprise in your purse for you," he chortled. I smiled and thought that it was some candies from the Cuban restaurant where we had eaten.[37]

My ghetto '93 Civic rattled at high speeds the whole way to my prince. Along the way, my phone dinged with a text message. I had tucked my phone into my purse and hadn't looked at it since leaving the restaurant with Julio, so I thought that maybe it was my Colombiano. I reached in my bag and skimmed my fingertips across two scratchy sounding, unfamiliar feeling objects. I confidently hoisted them out of my bag thinking it was candy trash. *Nope.* They were condoms. (I know what you're thinking, but even though I had already had sex, I had never officially touched a condom wrapper.) *Lovely.* I searched for my phone and discovered that the text was actually from Julio..."Enjoy!" I ignored his message and continued my trek onwards.

When I pulled into the parking lot, Colombiano wasn't waiting for me outside. I schlepped up the stairs of the grand fortress that held him captive once more before he was banished back to his *arepa*-yielding kingdom for an unknown amount of time. I knocked on the door of the towering prison. It creaked open, "*Hola.*" (Hello).

"*Hola. ¿Cómo estás? ¿Dónde está mi querido?*" (Hi, how are you? Where is my dearest?)

"*¡Ehhh Largo!*" (Hey Long! It was his nickname because he was tall.)

---

[36] Let's be honest—did I even know what good sex was? NO.

[37] I'm an idiot.

Colombiano peeped his head from the second story loft. His eyes lit up, and my heart dropped. He ran down the stairs and grabbed my hand to lead me up the tower, saying he had to finish packing before they left early the next morning. Colombiano sat me on the bed as he began folding the pile of clothes scattered over its surface and smashing them into his tiny suitcase. I smiled as I watched, thinking about the distance and how difficult it would be for us to be apart after being so perfect for each other. (Yup, still deranged.)

My Colombian Casanova had packed most of his speedos away when he began walking toward me. He got down on his knees where he was eye level with me and collided his lips against mine. He placed his hand on my shoulder and pushed me back onto the bed. All I could think about in this beautiful romantic moment were the two condoms in my purse that I had no intention of using and how weird it was that I was being pressured to have sex by a man who didn't even like girls.

[Insert long boring make out story. Use your imagination.]

We didn't have sex. In fact, those condoms stayed hidden in my purse for quite some time. I liked having them there (not because I needed backup protection because I was having SO MUCH sex); they served as a reminder to me of a beautiful man on a beautiful night. That night was the final night that I saw him before he left the States and went back to Colombia. The kisses were bittersweet as I imagined what life would be like once he left and it was just me. In some delirious way, those unused condoms were a memento of all of it.

I was crazed. Colombiano had returned home, and I had stayed here in the US. We promised to speak to each other every day, and in the beginning, he kept his word. I would like to clarify now that when I give someone my word, I do not break that promise. Apparently, that statement does not hold true for everyone.

We would talk on the phone, Skype (although Colombiano was always late for our date by a day or a week) and message each other back and forth on Facebook (although he would take days, if not weeks to reply).

Before he began to dwindle away, we had discussed me going to Colombia. I took this discussion seriously and started saving money like the Great Depression was up for a second coming. I should have known better, especially once my beloved began to speak to me less and less. Days of no reply turned in to weeks and then finally when he would respond, it was usually with some meaningless string of words. I was pathetic, and he was an ass, but I still had it in my head that I would see him in Colombia. I mean, I had spoken to his entire family over Skype, and we had all agreed on my spring arrival! So I bought my ticket.

Eventually my Colombian *burro* stopped responding to me altogether. *This is a problem.* I had dropped eight-hundred dollars on a ticket to Colombia to see him. I was scared something had happened, but I knew he was swamped with school and water polo, so I kept reassuring myself that he was "just busy."[38] Then, something remarkable happened: someone had tagged him in a picture on Facebook. It was his brother, his brother's girlfriend, Colombiano, and a girl that I had never seen before...though I did recognize her name. It was his ex-girlfriend's name. *Oh really?* Of course, I examined the picture with the intensity of a forensic investigator. My Colombiano's hand was placed very low on his "ex" girlfriend's back. Too low to be "just" friends. I was enraged and began freaking out about my ticket. I was nineteen, had just bought an eight-hundred-dollar ticket to a country where I thought I'd be reuniting with the love of my life, and I had just found out he was a chicken shit liar.

I cried. Colombiano had lied to me. He had FUCKING lied. Instead of just being a man and telling me he had gotten back with his ex-girlfriend, he let me buy an expensive ticket to a land far, far away. *That bastard!* Unfortunately for him, I grew up with a lying sack of shit for a father, so I can be very patient when I want to make my strike against a man. I waited...and I waited...and I waited some more. Then finally Colombiano wanted to Skype with me. On my end of the call was frigidity; on his end was this coy, pseudo-warmth. *What a fuckin' idiot.*

---

[38] If you haven't already figured this out, "just busy" is an excuse when a guy doesn't want to talk to you but he doesn't have the balls to tell you that he doesn't want to talk to you. You should never have more balls than a guy you're dating. He's probably a pussy.

"Hey Daxie." (Yeah, I still hate this nickname.)

"Hi."

"*Te ves muy bonita…*" (You look so beautiful.)

What, I don't always look beautiful? Jerk. "Great. How's the weather."

"Can you do me a favor?" He smirked.

"Yeah?" I said as dry as the Mojave Desert.

"Can you stand up and turn around for me?" He spun his lanky finger around on my computer's screen.

Sure. Can you stand up and sit your ass down on this finger. [Insert middle finger here.]

"Why?" I hissed.

"I want to see your wonderful butt."

"Oh, sure."

I stood up, didn't turn around and slammed my "wonderful" ass back down on my chair. *Thud.*

"Hey!" he shouted.

"What?" I gritted my teeth.

"I didn't see it."

"Oh, you didn't?"

"Eyy, Daxie, *no seas grosera.*" (Hey (name that I hate) don't be a brat.)

"Hmm…how's your girlfriend?" I shot at him.

SILENCE.

Colombiano wouldn't look at me. I had caught him. I had caught that dirty, lying bastard red-handed. I could see it in his eyes that he was trying to come up with an excuse, so I interrupted him before his broken words could percolate to his deceitful lips, "You know, I bought a ticket to Colombia because someone—YOU!—told me you wanted me to come out. YOU also told me you didn't have a girlfriend. So now I have this very expensive ticket, and NOW I don't know what to do with it."

"I'm sorry."

Of course, he was sorry, he had gotten caught. "Bye." I slammed my laptop shut.

True to form, I deleted all forms of social media. I had no reason to keep it. The only reason I had it, to begin with, was because of Colombiano, to stay in contact with a lying man. I had allowed myself to be blinded from all of the signs of his deceitful nature. I was nineteen and convinced that I had found my soulmate just because he fit some ridiculous criteria I had invented for myself. Lesson learned: Long distance doesn't work outside of movies.

My half-wit Colombian tried his hardest to redeem himself and began messaging my mom and sister to ask how I was, while I tried my hardest to get my money back on my plane ticket. He couldn't redeem himself, and I couldn't refund my money...win some, lose some. I had won his regret, and I'd lost a stack of hard-earned cash. I didn't need someone like Colombiano in my life, I had already dealt with a lying philanderer most of my life with my father, and I needed something more. So, I decided to focus on school and soccer and making real friends at home—which is to say I lost myself down the rabbit hole of more poor choices in boys...not men.

TWO YEARS TOO MANY

"Thunders"...hear the clap of my mighty thighs.

I told you I was husky for a bit, right? Well, meet the reason I lost weight—Hottie with the Body. He was 6'4", lean as hell, and tattooed. HWTB epitomized tall, dark and handsome. He was exactly what I needed (or so I thought). I saw him once, and I was hooked. 24-Hour Fitness was now my Mecca. For this reason and this reason only, I credit Hottie with the Body for my weight loss. Although he wasn't actively encouraging me to go to the gym, I couldn't miss a gym day with him if I was planning on him asking me out soon.[39] Easier said than done, of course, but I stuck to it. You can bet my once and still cellulite-ridden ass[40] that I worked out every day at noon. HWTB had to ask me out, I told myself, it was just a matter of time. I would not stop squatting and lunging until he was MINE!

Every day. Every. Damn. Day. I went to that gym, and every damn day Hottie with the Body would make eye contact with me. And every damn day he steered clear of me. I would call my mom at the end of every single gym session and give her a recap of how many times we made eye contact,[41] and the calls would pretty much go like this: She would cheerfully answer her phone, "Hi Nena."

"Hi, Mom," which usually came out as a moaning whine.

"How was Hottie with the Body?" (See even she knew his name.)

---

[39] See how that works?

[40] It's hereditary...sue me.

[41] I'm a psycho, and she enables me.

48

"Gahhhhh, he was so cute today. He came in with his scrubs and totally kept looking at me."

"That's good, Nena, did you do squats in front of him?" (Yes, my mom pimps me out.)

"Ugh! I just want him to ask me out already!"

"You should ask him ou—"

"Nah, he's going to ask me out." I wouldn't consider anything less than the scenario I'd been picturing while slaving (and drooling) on the elliptical.

The irony of that phone call (and maybe the lives of all daughters in history) is that Mama knew best. He didn't ask me out. In fact, I ended up asking him out in the weirdest and most awkward way my nineteen-year-old self could conjure up.

We saw each other nearly all the time and every day he would look at me and smile but never come up and talk to me. HWTB would linger around my workout area, but he would never take it a step further to open his mouth and speak words. *Why do you taunt me so?* I remember going to soccer practice and telling my teammates what a babe this gym guy was. I had no idea what his name was, but all I needed to know was that he was like Grade-A Man Meat. (Obviously I hadn't learned my lesson after Colombiano or the dipshits that followed after him.)[42]

Our stars finally aligned and the gods answered my prayers. One night after class and after my mom had gotten off work, I decided to be a good daughter and run errands with her. Let me tell you, karma has never been so giving. Our first stop in our series of errands was Bank of America. Mama pulled into a parking space directly in front of the bank, got out of the car, and started walking toward the front entrance of the bank. Just then a blacked out Mercedes pulled into the parking space to our right. From the corner of my eye, I saw a vision emerge from the driver's side. I squealed. It was Hottie with the Body. He looked right past me as he walked to the curb while I crazily tried to catch my mother's attention as she approached the front door of the bank. She ignored me, but he, unfortunately, saw my flailing arms and

---

[42] I think this all actually makes me a dipshit. I'm sure you're all catching on by now.

smirked. *Oops.* I sank into my seat, and my gut dropped to my butt. I was so embarrassed.

Hottie with the Body walked up to the ATM, completed his transaction and headed back to the parking lot all before my mother finished her business inside. As he walked back to his car, we caught eyes again. This time, he stood in front of my door and mouthed, "Hi."

I cautiously/ecstatically opened my door and said, "Hey, I see you at the gym all of the time."

"Yeah, it's just down the street from my work," he said, shuffling his feet from side to side.

"Oh, it's just down the street from my house. What do you do for work?" I was praying to god that HWTB would say he was a doctor. (I may or may not have been obsessed with *Grey's Anatomy* at this time and was on a hunt for my Dr. Shepherd.)

"Cool. I'm a vet tech."

"That's why you're always in scrubs!"

He chuckled. "I'm [Hottie with the Body], by the way."

"Nice to meet you, I'm Dax."

"Well Dax, I will make sure to say hi to you the next time I see you at the gym."

I giggled and probably turned bright red, "Okay, see you at the gym...Bye."

HWTB waved goodbye, I shut my door, and he ducked back into his car. I could not wait to workout next! Mama returned to the car, and I bombarded her with my crazed story of how I officially just met Hottie with the Body.

So it was only a matter of days before I got to talk to Hottie with the Body again. There I was on the leg extension machine really breaking a sweat when he came up to me to chat as he had promised just a few days before, "Hey, Dax!"

"Hi," I nearly shouted at him with a big fat grin on my face.

Our conversation began innocently enough, but then HWTB outweirded me. I know! I didn't think that this was humanly possible until he did it. He started to tell me how he had become so obsessed with working out after his car accident back in high school. It was a pretty serious accident in which he had broken his back, and the doctors predicted that he would never be able to walk again. He reiterated that his obsession with working out was because he had to keep his back strong. That's the sad part of his story; the weird part is coming in five... four...three...."I also broke my penis in the accident."

Now, I ask you—because I still don't know—HOW WAS I SUPPOSED TO FLIRT WITH AN OPENING LINE LIKE THAT??

"Don't worry," he quickly reassured me, probably because of the look on my face. And the fact that my eyes darted down to his groin. HWTB continued, saying that it was all healed up and normal. But between you and me, the bulge beneath his gym shorts was significantly hooked to the left...but that's just my naked opinion. I wasn't quite sure what to do with these tidbits, so I just nodded my head while he continued on with the rather serious and sad story of how he broke his back and his Johnson. In the middle of a very crowded 24-Hour Fitness. At full volume. Oddly enough, I was not turned off by his TMI.[43] I kind of liked it and saw him as an honest man who didn't care what people thought, which for me that was a breath of fresh air.

Our one-sided conversation came to a close and we both returned to our workouts. But HWTB still hadn't asked me out, even after he told me all about his broken penis...*I'm confused.* A couple of weeks went by at the gym and still nothing. Finally, I'd had enough. I was going to ask him for his number! Which I did in the dumbest, least forward way possible.

I had decided that since he was a vet tech and my cat had a litter of three kittens[44] (that's another long story for some other time), I would ask him about my cat. I remember walking up to him when he was in between rowing sets. It was awkward. I was awkward...but fuck, he was super awkward, so who cares...right?

"You sure are rowing hard there," I said, hooking my arm through the air.

"Oh, haha, yeah. Hey." His eyes lifted towards mine.

---

[43] That is not to say that I was not still wholesomely weirded out by his broken penis.

[44] Note: Cats are whores when they aren't fixed. Fix your cats as soon as you can.

"I was wondering..."

His face brightened for a second, "About?"

"So, you're a vet tech, and I have a whore of a cat who just had some kittens, and I was wondering if you would do a mommy checkup on her and her babies?" I spat the words out of my mouth like hot soup.

"Yeah, bring her by!"

"Thanks!" *Come on Dax ask for his number.*

"Is Thursday okay? I'll have more time to run through the checkup myself then," HWTB said standing up.

"Yeah, what's your number? I'll text you before I come in."

"Perfect! It's..."

My discombobulated fingers clumsily typed his number in to my phone. I couldn't believe I had just asked for his number. Now there was only one problem: I had to wait until Thursday to text him...*Oy vey.*

Thursday came and I confirmed my pussy's appointment (my *cat*... perverts) with HWTB. He kept texting me the rest of the day with stupid emojis, which I thought was cute. I have never in my life been so excited to take my cat to the vet. Hell, I was even taking my mom to the vet with me! It was going to be a big family outing so that Mama and the pussies could meet my future baby daddy.

Our appointment was set for 5:45 p.m. (since I had to wait for my mom to get off of work to "help" me round up the cats). In we waltzed, two women and four cats, "Hi, my name is Dax Marie, I have an appointment."

"Hmm, I don't see your appointment," the front desk girl snarled.

Then out walked HWTB, "I've got this Candice, this is my friend. I'm doing a mommy and kitten checkup for her." He looked toward me and smiled.

Oh yeah, you can do a checkup on me. "Hi [HWTB], this is my mom, and these are my kitties."

HWTB snickered and came around to give us all hugs (not my cats of course). He led us to the back of the office where their checkup rooms were. The appointment lasted all of fifteen minutes, but we stayed for another thirty after that just talking. We wrapped everything up, put the kitties back in their box and left. Again, he didn't ask me on a date or admitted his hot, undying love for me, or anything remotely close to it. We just said bye and that was that. My mom and I got back in the car and drove away as though that was just business. "He kept looking at you," she said. But I already knew that. What I didn't know was why he hadn't asked me on a damn date. I was putting myself out there, so why wasn't he closing the deal?!

By this time school had ended, and summer was in full swing. So on Thursday, July 5, I marched up to him at the gym and asked if he wanted to see *Ted* with me "because I had no one to go with."[45] He said yes, so I told him to text me (since I had deleted his number)[46]...I was done playing this pussyfoot game. We agreed to Sunday, July 8, since we both had that day off (but in actuality, I had switched my night shift for the day shift). He texted me sometime around three with "Hey" and a ♥. I pretended not to know who he was. (I thought it would keep him on his toes...but now I just think it was bitchy.)

I raced home from work, bragging to everyone along the way how I had a hot date with Hottie with the Body. My phone kept dinging the whole way home with emojis from him: ♥...🐱...👍. I was ecstatic. I hopped in the shower, scrubbed my body down and lotioned myself up...*Mama gotta smell good tonight!* Black pants (that I barely fit in to)[47] and this swingy lilac lace top. I curled my hair, smothered my face in makeup, and I was ready to go. The movie started at 7:45, and HWTB was scheduled to pick me up from my house at 7:00. He got there a little early, but luckily I was ready—I mean it's not like I was waiting by the front door.[48]

Aaaaaannnd we were off! We got to the mall and walked straight to the theater. He whipped out his wallet and bought our tickets. Since we still had time to kill, we walked over to Starbucks and got hot chocolates (he didn't drink coffee, and I didn't want to get freakishly caffeinated in front of him). We put the hot chocolates in my giant purse and

---

[45] That was a lie, and yes, that date is exact. Told you I was a psycho with dates.

[46] It's plain and simple. I delete numbers to avoid texting guys. Duh. I just tell them, "I forgot to save it." 😺

[47] Fat doesn't all come off at once.

[48] I was waiting by the front door.

waltzed into the theater with only a few minutes to spare. The theater was surprisingly crowded and we were forced to sit off to the side toward the front. The worst seats in the theater.

In all honesty, I did not want to see *Ted*. I thought the movie looked stupid, but I knew it was a guy's movie so I went with it. HWTB loved it. He had this laugh, this mouth-breather laugh that did not fit him at all. It made me laugh just hearing him laugh. His sense of humor was simpleminded, and I should've known then that we weren't meant to be, seeing as I enjoy the dark side—but he was hot and I was shallow and decided to ignore the inkling.

The movie carried on and so did my fantasies of HWTB. Once it ended, I gathered my things while Hottie with the Body gathered himself (since he had been laughing so hard) and we left. We walked back to his car talking about our plans for the future and saying little about our pasts, which I found a little strange but didn't want to put too much thought into it. I was having a decent time, hardly the time of my life, but I was out with a great looking guy and felt lucky to be there.

We pulled into my driveway and sat for another hour just talking. Hottie with the Body talked a lot that night. He told me about his car accidents (yes, plural), which were the apparent source of all his funds. He seemed to focus all of his attention on the fact that I spoke with my hands a lot, the way his "whole entire crazy Sicilian" family did. It seemed like some sort of comfort to him—that I reminded him of a giant, jubilant family.

But when HWTB actually spoke of his real family, he shut down. His face turned straight and his eyes glassed over as if he was inciting instructions to an audience of accountants. He emotionlessly told me of his father's death which occurred just after his big car accident (the one in which the doctors told him he'd be paralyzed), briefly mentioned his four siblings, and only spoke of his mother once. I found it strange that he spoke of his family in such a dispassionate manner, let alone how rarely he brought his family up in conversation. I always talk about my family…all of them…even when we aren't having the best of times.

I remember thinking to myself: *this poor guy has not had an easy life. He just needs someone to love him.*

HWTB fascinated me, but he also made me sad. He was lively and charismatic, but as time went on this wasn't always the case. In the beginning, he dominated conversation—not in a bad way. In fact, I barely spoke, which is a rarity for me since I usually don't shut up. I would ask him a question, and he would answer and answer and answer some more. His stories were never very detailed; they usually consisted of him talking about all of his "friends" and the things they had done but never anything that he had personally done. Oddly enough, I didn't find any of this to be alarming in the beginning.

As we started spending more time together, HWTB grew quieter. It was like the closer we became, the further away he pushed himself mentally. He hardly talked even though we were always together and if he did it was never serious. Now and then he would make some comment about how he grew up and then he would shut off.

On one of our first dates, he nonchalantly mentioned how the first time he had broken his nose was because of his father. I stopped doing what I was doing and scanned his face for emotion. There was nothing. He had said it in a way that was purely "matter of fact." In HWTB's eyes, it wasn't wrong, and it wasn't right; it just was. I would try to be supportive and ask a question or comment, but I was in way over my head. I had never personally dealt with this and never knew anyone who had grown up in such a way. I couldn't understand, and I wanted to help him, but I didn't know how. I didn't know then what I know now about the cycle of abuse and how it manifests itself through the generations of the abused and the abusers.

So it probably isn't fair for me to say that, as time unraveled, so did he, and that he was batshit nuts without even knowing it. We weren't friends, we weren't lovers and we never fought (because I'm a horrible human being and I start one-sided fights).[49]

Do you want to know what the weirdest part of all of this was? Hottie with the Body wouldn't kiss me. He *NEVER* kissed me. A few weeks in to us "dating" (I mean not dating? I don't know, I'm still confused by the matter), he hadn't kissed me. I was sincerely starting to

---

[49] His words not mine…I call bull 💩 on him.

think I had halitosis or that I was mentally deranged and making our relationship/the time we spent together up in my head.

According to Hottie with the Body, we were nothing, yet I couldn't talk to any other guy without him getting red in the face. I was pretty much forbidden from talking to my best friend Rambo (who is a straight, good-looking man and was also my workout buddy) without HWTB making some backhanded, passive aggressive comment to me later.

I remember one time when HWTB and I had gotten into some stupid fight (because that's what it always was, I would get fed up with him treating me a certain way and call him out on it, and then he'd kick me to the curb. Later, he'd beg for me to come back by saying, "I miss you," "I think about you all of the time," "Why did we stop talking?"). We weren't speaking to one another, and this time I was serious—I wasn't going to go back to him.[50] I had asked Rambo if he wanted to workout with me so I could talk about it with someone, and we set a different time to workout than what was normal for HWTB at the gym. But guess who showed up? Yup, in walked HWTB, looking pissed as all hell. Nothing was said, and I didn't even look his way, but of course he felt the need to text me: "Why're you getting workout advice from chicken legs?" I ignored him, but he kept blowing up my phone with emojis—☹…☹…☹. Then, after a few hours, HWTB's tone began to change back to sweet. So like always, I ended up back with him.

This cycle was endless. The jealousy at times was unbearable, and the name-calling was cruel. Since I played soccer and I was still working on losing weight, Hottie with the Body decided that my nickname should be "Thunders," as in short for thunder thighs. Even though I was still chubby, I never knew I had thunder thighs until he said it. When HWTB texted me, he rarely used words; instead, he would send me ⚡ to substitute for "Thunders." He would constantly remind me that my boobs were saggy (an unfortunate result of losing weight after gaining a lot of it, something of which I was already well aware) and the only nice thing about me was my ass because "it was big and in everyone's face."[51]

---

50 👎

51 🍑

HWTB would tell me that I talked too much, but if I didn't talk at all then he would say I was acting weird and he was going to take me home. He always wanted to pick me up from work, which at the time consisted of me being a hostess at a restaurant where I had to dress "like I was going out to the club" according to the owner's son (who was a pervert). Before I carry on, I would like to clarify now that I never dressed inappropriately. I would wear high heels and tighter dresses (as demanded by the pervert manager[52] who would otherwise tell me I looked Amish) that never showed a lot of skin.

One night, I remember HWTB coming to get me from the restaurant (he would never come inside and only announced his arrival through text) and telling me I looked like a slut because he could see through my tight knee-length black dress. "I can see your underwear. They're red. You look like a slut." I was wearing purple underwear, so I ignored him but couldn't stop worrying about how I looked after that. *Do I look slutty?*

If you're wondering why I would put up with treatment like this, you're right to question it. I wish I had asked more of those kinds of questions. Especially since I carried on with Hottie with the Body in this way for two years.

Why? Why did I do this? Two years of back and forth...that stupid, immature "breaking up" and "getting back together"[53] game, always being put down but somehow always being talked back up. The lows were so low and the highs felt so high. Though now that I can see that the highs were never so high. They just seemed high because I was always so low.

During my time with HWTB, I thought that I was nothing. I had thought of him as this god, someone who could do no wrong, and I would allow myself to be persuaded that he knew best and I knew nothing. Everyone that knew him thought he was this stand-up guy. Even my mom would always tell me that I was overreacting and

---

[52] He is a walking sexual harassment violation.
[53] I would like to reiterate that we didn't actually break up or get back together since Hottie with the Body "would never date me." Note: I was obviously 🙂 by his 😫 and 🍆.

how sweet he was. Somehow, I had convinced myself that I could out-love all of the badness in HWTB's life—the death, the abuse, the abandonment. I allowed myself to be brought down because I thought I could save him. The sickest part of all of this is that I may have stayed with him had it not been for one professor.

Some time toward the end of my and HWTB's non-relationship, I took a psychology class. It was my first class of the day in a big hundred-person lecture hall. Every day, I'd get to class early to read up on the previous material and avoid the parking fiasco that occurred at a certain time before classes started. I began to chitchat with my professor every morning. At first, we wouldn't talk about much except for the day's lesson or how I thought the class was coming along, but then one day I decided to ask him more about the current section we were working on.

The focus of this portion of the class was abnormal psychology under which falls narcissism. He had explained narcissism—what it was, what the signs and symptoms were and what the causes are believed to be—a few days earlier, and a lot of it sounded familiar. Somewhere in the midst of him addressing the signs and symptoms, I remember thinking, *oh, my god, this is HWTB*. Everything about my beautiful Hottie with the Body screamed wrong. He constantly berated my thoughts and feelings, nearly ostracized me from my friends and rarely showed emotions of his own except when they had a sexual connotation. For so long I had felt like something was not right, but I had been convinced otherwise, that something was not right with *me*.

Later that night, my intense research began. I wanted to know if I was crazy and this was all coincidental, or if this unfortunate personality disorder would explain why HWTB was the way he was and treated me the way he did. I armed myself with a plethora of knowledge and prepared myself to ask my professor specific questions.

The following class, I walked into the lecture hall with heavy shoulders but a mostly heavy heart. I didn't want anything to be wrong with HWTB, but couldn't deny that the description fit him to a tee. It would explain a lot. Moreover, I thought that maybe a diagnosis would allow him to get help. I began asking my professor the myriad of questions I had prepared, but he quickly realized that I was asking these questions for personal reasons. "Why don't you make an appointment during my office hours so we can go more in-depth with these answers?" he suggested in a concerned manner. I agreed, and we set an appointment for a few days out.

When the day arrived, I already knew what his answer would be. We spoke for about an hour on the matter. From a professional standpoint, he said that he would need to see HWTB in person to give him a proper diagnosis. He added that, based on what I had told him, Hottie with the Body seemed to fall under the category of narcissism; however, narcissism works on a moving scale, and to some extent, everyone is slightly narcissistic.

My biggest take away from this meeting with my professor was that something like this, like narcissism, usually develops as a coping mechanism. This means that HWTB would have developed this sometime during childhood as a means to cope with his not always picturesque upbringing. Moreover, someone like him may never realize anything is wrong; therefore, he most likely would never seek or accept treatment.

The hardest part of all of this? My professor told me, "He may likely never change." A flood of thoughts and emotions raced through my overthinking head. *What do I do? Is he sad? Does he know I care? Does this have to be the end? Does he know that he is missing out on a whole big, beautiful life?*

Still, I stayed a while longer with HWTB. I thought I could do something, that I could help. I believed that with the knowledge I had in my back pocket that I could avoid the fighting and mind games. I thought I could "save" him. But I fell short.

I couldn't keep the fights at bay for long, and the cruelty of his words and actions began to fly above head like vultures again. I tried. God, I tried. I really wanted it to be better, even if I wasn't there for him. I'm not perfect, I'm not a doctor, and I'm only as smart as my experiences lead me to be. So one day, I left, and I didn't turn back. Here I was, this almost twenty-one-year-old girl still searching for herself, getting lost in a man who may never realize he's lost, too.

I had to leave. The fights were wearing, the emotions were turning to hate, and all I wanted was to help this guy who never knew he needed help. I had to leave. I had to. I was about to transfer to a four-year university and didn't need the distraction of a hapless heartache because the guy I "wasn't" dating told me I looked slutty in something I was wearing, or because he "forgot" we had plans, or some other bullshit thing he would do because he was scared of actually admitting to himself that he cared for me. I needed to be ONLY ME. I NEEDED to focus on ME. I was done being broken. I wanted to be loved and to love. I no longer wanted to be trapped by what I thought love was.[54]

I finalized us the only way I knew how: I blocked and deleted HWTB's number.[55] Yes, I blocked his number! I blocked it because I knew if I didn't I would fall trap to the games again and I deleted it because that once-perfect numerical heptad was too dangerous for me in my phone. I only wanted to feel needed, and HWTB knew precisely how to do that when he wanted to come back.

At the time, I was mentally weak, and it wasn't only because of him. I was young and lacking in experience. I never had an exemplary relationship between my parents to model my future relationships after. I was angry and immature, and I wanted to feel accepted…In short, I was the perfect girl to get caught up in someone like HWTB. I was shallow and insecure which was the perfect combination for a tremulous "non" relationship. Please don't think I am blaming any of my negative experience on him or my parents; I'm not. I am merely stating the facts of where I was mentally at the time. Now, if someone like HWTB came into my life, I would be able to walk away and not do the same stupid dance.

Summer of 2013 came and went. I had been accepted to a four-year university and would begin classes later that September. In honor of my milestone twenty-first birthday and my acceptance to such a grand university, I decided to dye my hair brown (because, you know, this is what every girl does when she needs a "change" in her life). I figured

---

[54] I still had a long ways to go before I actually understood love/my self-worth.

[55] What? You can block and delete a number from your phone? Yes. Yes, you can.

the brown hair matured me, made me look more studious...it just "changed" me.

So, with brown hair, I started classes at my big name university, and for the first time in forever, I was my sole focus. I wasn't caught up in guys or how I looked (besides the change in hair color)...I just was. My thoughts of Hottie with the Body slowly began to trickle away, and eventually, I barely thought of him. I started to do things for myself without considering who would approve of what I was doing. I was all I had to worry about. School, traffic (since I commuted from Orange County to L.A. every morning), work, yoga and eating healthy. (Whoa, baby, I was so committed to the new me.)

I was permanently exhausted from my new schedule. I would wake up at 4:30 a.m. four times a week, leave my house by 5:00 a.m. and get to yoga in Downtown L.A. no later than 6:00 a.m. From yoga, I would go to Korea Town to the gym to shower and maybe do a little cardio, then travel farther down Wilshire to Beverly Hills to get coffee and breakfast and finally arrive on campus sometime between 8:30 and 9:00 a.m. Depending on the day, I had class until 2:00 p.m., then afterward, I would always rush back home to my assistant job and occasionally my waitressing job after that...so it's no wonder HWTB began to barely cross my sleep-deprived brain. Of course, that was about to change. About nine weeks into my first quarter, HWTB popped back into my brain...like a zit. But luckily for me, I had a great skincare routine going for me.

It was later on a Saturday night, and I was working the front desk of the restaurant. I had gone to the patio area to seat someone, and when I looked up, there he was on the other side of the fence, just staring at me. His eyes said something different than what they were normally colored. They said hope.

"Enjoy your dinner," I said to the customers as I ran back inside. *Am I crazy? That was him, right? Was he actually just out with one of his friends or rolling solo?* I tried to remain calm as I tripped back up to the front desk. Seconds went by, eventually totaling minutes which eventually led to Hottie with the Body walking into the restaurant (something he would've never done in the past) and coming in to say "hi" (which he also would've never done) and introducing me to his friend (which he would have absolutely never done). We sat in the front of the emptying restaurant and chatted back and forth (also, something that never happened/used to be one-sided...Correction: me-sided).

HWTB stared at me while I stared at his friend. I didn't know how to take all of him in...his whole demeanor had seemed to change. He wasn't the guy I had blocked some months ago. He was a salvaged man.[56] The clock ticked by ticking them on their way out, but before they left, HWTB asked me if he could text me after I got off of work.

"Yeah," I cooly said, acting as if it didn't faze me.

"Alright, I'll text you in a bit. Maybe you can come out with us afterward?" He said it as if he was scared to ask me.

"Maybe. I have a lot of studying to do," I retorted back defensively but unsure.

"Oh, okay. Bye."

"Bye."

What the hell am I doing? I thought as I unblocked his number from my phone (yes, I still knew which number was his even after it was blocked and deleted). Minutes later, a text came in, "It was nice seeing you. You look good with dark hair," punctuated with ♡. I ignored him like he had done so many times before to me.[57]

My head was a mess. I had worked so hard to "get away" from Hottie with the Body but now it was like he was walking up to me and saying sorry. I didn't know what to do, so I didn't do anything. I ate dinner at the restaurant, grabbed my car from the valet, drove myself home and got ready for bed. All of the sudden my phone was bombarded with texts from HWTB. He was at the dive bar down the street from my house, and he wanted me to come out with him and his friend. I told him no. There was no question about it. It was a plain and straight no, but his texts continued and became all the more sweet with wishing I was there and pleading with me. Eventually, I caved. I figured what the hell, I was twenty-one, it was a Saturday night and it

---

[56] No, he was not.

[57] 🖕

was just before midnight...I had plenty of time to get there and come back in fifteen minutes if I decided so.

I got to the shithole excuse for an Irish pub and was greeted by HWTB. A big, warm hug. "Come inside, let's find Joe," he excitedly exclaimed as he grabbed my hand and wove me through the crowd of drunk bros. Joe was drunk as could be at the bar looking for his "in" to order another drink while HWTB appeared to still be in his sorts.

Joe's face lit up, "[HWTB] has been talking about you nonstop! Let me get you a drink." He and I walked down the bar top to order a drink while HWTB stood his ground to save our spots at the table he had just found. Joe and I ordered only him a drink and returned to our table to see HWTB getting hounded by some girl who clearly and uncouthly wanted his nuts. *Whatever, he's not mine and I don't care.*[58]

The bar was closing, and it was time to go. The three of us, leaving the nut-hungry bimbo behind at the bar, began walking back to my car. We piled in, and I drove them back to Joe's house with plans to leave straight from there back to my own home. WRONG! I remained seat belted in as HWTB and Joe unbuckled and exited my car. Suddenly, my inebriated HWTB realized my car wasn't turning off and that I wasn't getting out, so he asked me to come inside. "No, I can't. I have to wake up early in the morning to study," I lied.

Then Joe popped up behind him, "Come on, let me get you a drink. Just ONE and then you can leave." I reluctantly agreed. I was scared because I had worked so hard to get over HWTB and now here I was like a sitting duck, deciding to go into a house with him. I was terrified. I still wanted him so badly after eight months of having nothing to do with him.

The house was quiet and cold. Joe's roommate was dead asleep, so we went outside on the balcony to avoid interrupting his peaceful slumber. We positioned ourselves around the tiny patio, Joe on a big lounger while HWTB and I crowded the love seat. I sat on one end, trying to avoid the nauseating accidental grazes of our bodies while he continued to scoot in closer to me.

---

[58] LIAR! I totally cared. 🔫🙍...oops.

Joe talked and talked and talked while I listened in attempt to occupy my brain with anything except HWTB. Suddenly, Joe realized that none of us had drinks and abruptly left us alone to grab some. The door to the balcony slid shut, and HWTB turned to me, "I'm so glad you're here." I smiled, I didn't know what to say, and I still had no idea how to feel toward him. Without warning, he engulfed me in a hug, "I miss you so much."

"I have to leave," I interrupted.

"Don't say that."

"I can't do this. I shouldn't be here," I said trying to talk some sense into myself.

"Please stop, I'm sorry."

I stopped. I looked at HWTB's face, hoping to find it written in lies, but I failed to see even a wrinkle of insincerity. He seemed like a completely different person. It was as though he was trying to give me his drunken heart…the same heart that I had been searching for so many months ago. Just then, the door to the balcony slid back open delivering us with Joe and drinks. Hottie with the Body nuzzled his lips to my ear, "I think about you all of the time." I melted in spite of myself.

We sat huddled together on that numbing December night on a tiny balcony as he and his friend entertained me with stories of their childhood and their long-lasting friendship. HWTB would hug me in tighter with each laugh. The night seemed to go on forever when only a couple of hours had passed. I kept telling myself that I needed to go home, that I needed to find the perfect opportunity to get myself out because I couldn't allow myself to fail like this again.

The stories began to fade to silence just as Joe's sobriety completely escaped him. HWTB shooed him off to his bed, and I gathered myself to leave. He stopped me: "Please don't go, I don't think it's safe for you to drive." I hadn't even had a quarter of my glass of wine.

"I need to go," I replied.[59]

"It's late," he coaxed.

---

[59] Me to Myself: You 👏 need 👏 to 👏 go 👏!

"I'm fine." But I sounded as though I was reassuring myself more than him.

"I want to try this again."

Once again, I looked to HWTB's face to find the lies, and again I found nothing but sincerity.

"Please, baby, let's start over." (He never called me baby.)

"I'm not sleeping with you," I growled.

"I don't want you to, I just want to be next to you." And again nothing but truth spewed from his lips and stained his face.

We walked hand in hand to the bedroom. We had never spent the night together, and I was overwhelmed with self-judgments and imaginations of us. HWTB stripped down to his boxers and handed me a shirt to sleep in. I turned it down and kept my clothes on. He grabbed extra blankets in case I got cold, turned off the light, and held me tightly. This was almost everything I had wanted, and now he was giving it to me.

Then, he turned my head to face his, and he kissed me. Now I had everything I wanted. His kisses were at first small, passionate bits of his love and then they became longer and harder, beating truthfully with his gushing heart. He was everything I ever wanted him to be at that moment. Our kissing progressed as our clothes slipped off. I wasn't scared anymore; he was the man I had always known he could be. He covered my mouth and whispered words of affection to me as my eyes filled with tears at the fruition of my long awaited wishes.

When we awoke the next morning, we were entangled. Wrapped together, my legs intertwined with HWTB's and his arms pulling me tightly into his body. This was the truth I had always known to be hidden somewhere deep down in his sorrowful soul. It was like clockwork, as though our bodies were completely in sync.

We both fumbled back into consciousness. I looked at my phone for the time, got dressed, and thought that maybe this was all in my head and that I had made a mistake and would walk out alone. I was wrong. HWTB walked me to my car with his arms around my waist and kissed me goodbye, "Text me when you're done studying."

I still couldn't believe the man that was holding on to me, "How about you text me when you charge your phone."

He responded with a kiss and "I'll talk to you in a bit," and then, he gently shut my door and waved me off as I drove down the street.

True to his new self, Hottie with the Body texted me later. We carried on the conversation for days only this time he didn't use emojis; he used words. But soon I wanted more than words. I wanted the body that delivered these new words. And when I asked to hang out with him, HWTB began coming up with excuses and, true to his old self, he started playing games.

Two weeks later, he came into MY restaurant and asked if I could get him a table for two. I was befuddled. Behind him stood a muscular, burnt orange girl (she looked like a man) in a horrendous, barely-there orange dress. I was devastated and so disappointed in myself. I sat them at a shitty table and watched as HWTB wined and dined this bodybuilder woman. *FUCK him*. I didn't need to block him from my phone; all I needed was to delete him. I had no need or desire to text him after that.

He left the restaurant and texted me "thanks."

I responded with a "fuck you" and "you're a pig," and like his old self, he didn't understand why I was mad.

Hottie with the Body—we were never meant to be and never should have been. He was beautiful and tainted, and I was young and naive. I wanted love, and he wasn't capable of love. Some days I do think of him. Occasionally, I see him at the gym, and we'll nod but rarely speak.

He unknowingly broke me down but made me stronger, too. After him, I began to see what I was worth (not all at once but slowly). I began to understand who I was and what I wanted. Of course, I was not perfect in these realizations, but his brokenness mixed with my brokenness created strength in me. Hottie with a Body is a soul that I will always hope the best for—from a distance.

VIVA LA HEARTBREAK PART 2

Because I obviously didn't get
enough the first time around.

My first year at my big name university flew by. The summer was quickly approaching, and I hadn't any plans except for those consisting of summer school and studying at the beach (and maybe hanging out with the new guy I had just started dating).[60] I wanted the summer before going in to my final year of university to be smooth and productive. I had signed up for four eight-week summer courses to get a head start on my medical school plans. Instead of doing an extension program at my current university, I had made the decision to study at the community college down the freeway from my home. This plan would save me oodles of money and most likely save a little more of my sanity since I wouldn't have to trek through traffic. My schedule was quite the load with classes four days a week, almost all day—and this was just the beginning of this new plan. In one summer I had decided to take on macro and microbiology with a microbiology lab and trigonometry. I figured, *why not overload myself now?*[61]

Not only had I decided to take on this heavy academic load but I had also decided to start dating a new guy, one who was also a heavy load.[62] Like Hottie with the Body and all of the magnificent predecessors that

---

[60] I know, I swore off men in the last chapter but obviously I swear them off all of the time. Are you starting to see the pattern?

[61] Because I am an overzealous psycho.

[62] No, I do not mean fat…although maybe he was slightly husky.

came before him, Daddy's Boy was a bad choice. However unlike all of those that came before him, I recognized his psychoses quite quickly and knew when to run (and believe me when I say I ran so fast and so far that I ended up in Colombia).[63] But before we move on to that mistake, the Colombian one, let's meet this mistake.

Backtrack with me…all the way back to May. My spring quarter of my first year was coming to a close. I had one week left of classes and then it was summer vacation (which for me meant more classes but closer to home). For one of my classes, my professor had benevolently decided to skip an in-class final but maliciously replaced it with a take-home final with a ridiculous set of criteria.

I had been working on this bastard of a project for the past two weeks. It was five separate essays exploring various topics of contemporary Argentina's history written entirely in Spanish with minimal (meaning no) grammar mistakes otherwise, you would be marked down (significantly because she was a Spanish dictator). Needless to say, I was a wreck with this final. I wanted an A and already knew what an impossible grader she was since I had already experienced her grading wrath in one of her other classes the quarter before. So to properly dedicate time to this final, I scheduled myself to work on it every day with workout breaks in between each couple of hour increments of writing and researching. That being said, I had just finished a six-mile run and settled on Starbucks to continue writing.

Starbucks was full but not packed. I found a table and sat my sweaty (and probably smelly) self down. I began cranking out an essay about Eva Peron's influence on the working class vote. The words were coming to me so easily. Honestly, I couldn't stand the subject matter of the essay because I thought Eva Peron was obnoxious—but for some reason (likely the mixture of endorphins and sweet, sweet caffeine), I was on a roll.

There I was type, type, typing away, totally in the zone and with nothing to distract me. I was only a few minutes into writing, but my music was perfect, my research was phenomenal, and my grammar was

---

[63] Possibly another mistake?

impeccable. Nothing could stop me. I was going to finish that essay right then and there. Alas, I was wrong. From underneath my bowed down head and tilted baseball cap, I kept seeing this waving motion. *What the hell is that? Whatever. Don't look up.* I looked up. I shouldn't have. There he was, that oversized spoiled brat of a man—Daddy's Boy.

Daddy's Boy had been frantically waving his hand at me in the middle of a meeting with a client signing documents. I looked up, smiled that polite passerby smile, and walked up to grab my vanilla latte from the bar. Daddy's Boy ran up to meet me there. "Hey," he said with a creepy, overzealous smirk on his face.

"Hi," I retorted scanning his face and appearance. *Cute-ish. Not hot.*

"Did you just work out?" he asked me with an ecstatic emphasis on "work out."

"Yeah. I ran."

"Wow, you're a runner?" He said it like it was hard to believe.

"Mhmm, sometimes."

"How many miles did you do?"

"Six." With that, I started turning back to my table.

"Whoa! Six!? I can tell you're in shape. Your legs look strong."

Ew. "Thanks. Have a nice day."[64]

I shut him off before he stepped over that fine line between complimentary and creepy. Don't get me wrong, I was flattered that he was flirting with me, but he was also kind of embarrassing me by doing it in front of his client and the Starbucks baristas who were all watching.[65]

I walked back to my table, put my headphones on and began working again. Only my concentration was not so concentrated on my essay because someone decided to continue to wave and whisper to me. (Okay fine, I will admit that it was kind of cute.) As his client was signing something serious—life insurance documents, I think—DB was waving and pointing to my big name university hat, mouthing that he liked it. He kept giving me thumbs ups and winking and

---

[64] "Have a nice day" is girl talk for "fuck off."
[65] Note: I am not being a narcissist.

obnoxiously trying to carry on the conversation as I was clearly working on something and he should have been focused on his client.

I would acknowledge him and then try to carry on with my essay but found it impossible. Especially when I had managed for a five-minute span to ignore him while his client asked him questions and then he shouted across his client and another table to ask, "Hey what's your number? I want to take you out." What was I supposed to do? Deny him in front of all of these people who were now watching us?[66] Embarrassed but again flattered by his zealous nature, I gave him my number. Then I sat for a few moments longer while he input my digits into his phone and sent me a text to verify that I had given him the real thing and not some rejection hotline.[67] Seconds later, Daddy's Boy got a phone call and stepped outside, so I took that as my cue to make an Irish exit of my own.

A quick note about Irish Exits, also known as the most flawless exit strategy in the world: This wordless, ideally unnoticed departure is a hallmark of my social skill set. If it takes ten thousand hours to achieve mastery of a skill, then I'm the goddamn Beethoven of leaving without saying goodbye. What Oscar Wilde did for the English language, I do for the Irish exit.

DB texted me shortly after I slipped out of Starbucks and formally invited me to dinner the following week. And even though he was slightly (only slightly) annoying when we met, I thought that he would be less obnoxious on a date when he didn't have to fight with an unwritten final essay for my attention. I was so wrong.

The night came for our big date and, for the most part, I was excited. There was something kind of obnoxious about him to me. He was a repeat texter. You know, those people that you don't respond to right away, so they respond to themselves by either re-sending you the same text or sending you a newly worded message that says the same thing. Sometimes people just don't understand that other people do

---

[66] Yes.

[67] Or you can give an ex's number (you know you remember at least one). You're welcome.

have lives outside of their phones. It obviously didn't occur to DB that I would purposely not text him back. Little did he know that it was for his own good—I didn't want to get burnt out on him before we even went on a date, so I would make him wait a bit and test his patience.

So our date was set, and Daddy's Boy picked me up from my house and drove us to the peninsula where he had chosen a nice restaurant with seating on the water and an even nicer wine list. As we pulled up to the valet, I had noticed his cupholders were chock full of change. I happened to grab one coin that was slightly larger than the rest, "Oh, that's my one year chip."

"Your what?"

"I've been sober for almost two years now."

"Sober?" *Oh fuck. I can't date an addict.*

"Yeah, I go to AA and NA five days a week. I post it on my Facebook."

Fuck. "Wow, good for you. I rarely ever have Facebook." (I had just put it back up.)

"Does that bother you?"

No, it's so wonderful that you go to Narcotics Anonymous. "No."

"Really? You seem bothered by it." He guessed correctly.

"So, no alcohol?" I asked.

"Not a drop. Are you sure this doesn't bother you?"

"My dad's an addict—maybe you've met him at a meeting when it's been court-ordered," I joked.

"Yeah, maybe I have. I want to be a sponsor one day." He responded, completely ignoring my joke.

DB obviously didn't understand my sarcasm, but what the hell? I was trying to stay away from addicts, and there I was, walking into a restaurant on a date with one.[68] So when the time came for the server to ask what we'd be having to drink, I froze up. *Is he still tempted by alcohol*

---

[68] Look, I know that his addictions should not and do not define him, but I also know from experience that addicts usually have certain pestilent personality traits that I do not want to be associated with. Sorry, that's just the truth.

if I drink it? How difficult was this year of sobriety? Will he be offended if I order a drink? Will he think I'm a lush?

"I'll take a Coke. Go ahead, you can order a glass of wine if you'd like," he urged from across the table.

"No, I'm okay," I assured him, too scared of the temptation that I posed.

"I saw you looking at the menu. Just order it. I won't be offended." He sounded pretty convincing.

"You sure?" I asked in one last attempt to avoid the awkwardness of drinking with a barely sober man.

"I'll be offended if you don't."

Problem solved. "The Rombauer Chardonnay, please," I said as I handed the wine list back to the server, and the night carried on unhitched.

DB told me everything. He told me how his addiction to heroin started, how he almost died, how his family was so supportive of him, what an amazing man his father was, and how he had just started his job selling insurance plans. He talked and talked, telling me stories of tragedy and success. He was leaving no rock unturned. It was great to hear someone speak so openly of their trials and tribulations in life. He was a nice change of pace from Hottie with the Body.

You know what I liked best about Daddy's Boy? I liked that he didn't back down from me when I was clearly bothered by his one year chip. I liked that he kept going even when I shut off for a few seconds, contemplating the significance of his chip. Our date wasn't fantastic, but it went better than expected. I switched from wanting to run away from yet another addict (the first being my father) to seeing a man who had fought his demons and was now making the most out of his second chance. At the end of the night, I appreciated DB for all that he was and wasn't. Our date ended, and he drove me back home with plans to see each other again soon.

That night was our only date. We saw each maybe three times after that but very briefly. DB's excuse being some challenge at work that he needed to win in order to be promoted (understandable) or the AA and NA meetings he attended five times a week (also understandable). But

what was unacceptable was not setting aside any time for this girl—
that's me—who he was just getting to know.

I understood his work thing, and I got that his AA/NA meetings
had to come first, BUT—and I know this sounds awful—I couldn't
understand why he had to go nearly every day. DB had no time for
me except for the couple hours that he could "spare" to see me, and
even then he would complain about how tired he was. *Bastard, I am in
summer school and working double shifts as a waitress when I can. Don't
bitch to me about being tired.* I was kind of getting fed up with him.
Daddy's Boy would text me nonstop but would never set time aside to
interact with me in person. Our whole relationship was founded and
developed through texts.

Well, it was only a matter of time before shit hit the fan. I had
just gotten off of work on a Sunday night. I was so busy, I barely had
any time to look at my phone, let alone answer text messages. DB had
sent me numerous texts—apparently, he wanted me to call him or
something. Just kidding, he DEMANDED that I call him. *Okay?* So
I called him, "Hi, what's up? Sorry, I just got off of work," I chirped.

"You're a liar."

"What?" I asked confusedly.

"You're a liar!" DB was shouting. I could feel his neck veins pulsing
through the phone.

"What did I lie about?" I was sincerely unaware of why he was so
angry or what I even "lied" about.

"You have Facebook."

"Yes, I have Facebook. What does that have to do with this?"

"You lied. You told me you didn't have Facebook."

"No I didn't."

"Yes, you did! I bet you have Tinder too."

"No, I didn't. I told you I rarely have Facebook," I corrected.

"No you didn't. You're a liar. You're probably on Tinder."

"I have never used Tinder," I huffed.

"How can I trust you now when I know you're a liar?"

"You're being ridiculous. I'm not arguing with you." I was surprising
myself with how calm I remained.

"BECAUSE YOU'RE LYING!" He screamed. I could hear the spit flying out of his mouth.

Now he was starting to piss me off. I'm no liar. I remained calm and shut the conversation down. I was not about to waste my time when I had not lied about anything. DB mentioned Facebook once and I commented once about it, but he had never directly asked me if I currently had it. I was rarely on the damn thing, so I didn't care if we were friends or not. Plus, we had only been hanging out for a couple of months and to be honest, the relationship was going nowhere. Daddy's Boy was too enveloped by his work and his meetings. I had nothing to lose if this already shitty "relationship" ended.

"I am not a liar."

"Really? Seems like you are. I bet you're fucking other guys."

God, you are a fucking idiot. "I know what I am and what I am not."

"I can never trust you."

Great because you've just proven yourself to be a psycho. "Great. You can believe and do whatever you want because, honestly, I don't care."

"How can you say that to me when I took you on a nice, EXPENSIVE dinner date."

"You took me on ONE date. ONE. Not two. Not three. ONE!"

"I took you on a nice—"

"And expensive dinner. I know, so expensive. Gosh, you must be broke from that one date. I mean, in the six weeks we've been talking and not hanging out, that sure is one big expensive date." The sarcasm flew over his head. DB was a blubbering idiot.

"I'm disappointed in you," he said in a last ditch effort to try to get me to change.

Oh darn, I'm going to go cry about it. "Talk to me when you calm down. Bye." I hung up the phone and knew that I was done with him. I didn't lie. I don't lie. I stopped talking to him. I was waiting for an apology, but I wasn't holding my breath and wasn't going to trust DB after he blew up at me for seemingly nothing. Without a doubt, it was time for me to move on.

Daddy's Boy tried to redeem himself after his little temper tantrum, but I wanted nothing to do with him. Three days later, after he calmed down, he tried to talk to me as though nothing had happened. He said he wanted to make it up to me and was sorry and yadda yadda yadda. I made him wait of course for my response.

I didn't want to hang out with his psycho ass anytime soon. I was "focusing" on school and spending time with my cousin and her new baby girl. I was just SOOOOO busy that I didn't have time for an unwanted date with a spoiled brat who wouldn't have his networking connections if it weren't for his daddy. Plus, I was still wondering whether I was wrong to judge him for his angry outburst against me.

No more than a week later did I make my decision final when I got a message. An unsolicited and unexpected message through Facebook. I was at my cousin's house in Long Beach visiting with her and her chubby-cheeked baby when I finally checked my Facebook and saw that some Dipshit Baby, I mean Daddy's Boy had friend requested me (yeah, even after that big hissy fit he threw and even after I was ignoring him), but more importantly, someone from a certain South American country had messaged me announcing his return to the United States.

I was fired up. I stared at the unopened message. *What could Colombiano possibly say to me? Does he really think he can just waltz back into this country and see me? Does he not remember what he did the last time? Is he an idiot too? Should I go to his game? No, I shouldn't. I should make him beg for it. What should I do?* I finally opened the message after a few seconds ticked by echoing thoughts of madness in my mind.

My eyes began to decode the not so broken English. It was honest, it was heartfelt, it was apologetic without apologizing, and it was everything that I never imagined it to be. Colombiano had written the message days before, on the day of his arrival, and I was reading it days later, almost a week after his return. Although my heart was warm and dancing in my chest, my mind told me to be still. I responded back to him bluntly, but seconds later he wrote back with an invitation to watch him play at Long Beach State, which just so happened to be two miles from my cousin's house. What are the odds?

I contemplated going. I swished the idea of me doing something potentially very romantic or ridiculously stupid in my head. I couldn't decide what to do. So I broke my silence, and asked my cousin. She looked at me like I was crazy, as though I shouldn't have even questioned it and I should have just gone. My cousin (who's really more of a best friend) told me to go, so I kissed her and her cherub goodbye and I left.

I arrived at the school much too quickly. I panicked; I couldn't be on time! I drove around a couple of times to stall myself from being timely.[69] I parked my car in the farthest parking structure possible as a means to delay my long-awaited reunion with a heartbreaking man. I parked on the highest level of the structure and walked down the stairs to the ground level. My brain was bubbling with bids of possibilities when I took a step off of the curb and heard it—a whistle and a "Daxie." My brain sank to my butt. I turned. There he was, looking as handsome as ever in his warm-ups with a posse of his teammates behind him. I smiled and stopped to let Colombiano catch up to me.

He jogged over in his sandals and perfectly tousled hair. Colombiano hooked his arms around my waist and hugged me tightly. "I'm so glad you're here," he said in perfect English with his endearing accent. He walked as I flew to the pool. He filled my ears with gratitude and compliments and stories of his life back home. He asked me about my family and school. It was like we were old friends catching up, only I never wanted to be his friend. We finally arrived at the pool and parted ways as he continued to the locker room, and I found myself a spot on the metal bleachers.

With thirty minutes to the start of the game, I called my mother in disbelief of what I was doing. She responded with, "I know, he messaged me a couple of months ago to tell me that he was coming back to the US and wanted to see you but he wanted to surprise you. I figured you would see him again even though you were upset." We chatted for some couple of minutes and then she had to get back to work. We hung up, and I waited for the men to come back out. I watched as Colombiano and his teammates poured out of the locker room, each of them looking my way. I watched as he glanced up at me and jumped into the pool

---

[69] Being on time is one of my biggest pet peeves and sometimes being so timely faults me. It's like my body won't let me be late and it's hard to make a fashionably late statement.

with a smile on his face. I watched the game unfold with ease as they creamed the Long Beach team. I watched them exit the pool and trickle back into the locker room. I watched as they waltzed back out of the locker room and I watched in suspense as Colombiano strolled back up to me on the benches, "Hey, my California girl."

"*Eyy, mi tonto colombiano.*" (Hey, my stupid Colombian.)

He grabbed my hand to lead me off of the bleachers and out of the pool area, but I pulled it away. "Hey, be nice, Daxie," he said embarrassed.

"Believe me, that *is* nice," I chuckled.

"Eyyyy! Thank you for coming to see me play."

"You're welcome." I didn't know what else to say.

"Will you come back to watch?" he asked.

"I don't know," I said completely honest.

Colombiano hugged me. That "I don't know" said a lot, and he knew why I didn't know. He began to apologize for what he had done almost three years before. I stared blankly at him as sorries circled his tongue and distrust dressed my heart. I didn't know what I wanted. On the one hand, he was giving me exactly what I had wanted, but on the other, I had already experienced his lies firsthand and thought I should know better than to trust a cheating man. He must have seen the rumination rummaging through my mind, so he did the only thing he thought possible. Colombiano kissed me.

"What're you doing?" I pushed him back.

"I wanted to kiss you."

"You can't kiss me."

"Why not? Do you have a boyfriend?"

I paused. I questioned his question, *Do I have a boyfriend? No, no I do not. I have a psycho that I am not talking to, and I guess I need to officially tell that I'm done with him.*

"Not really. Well, I was going to break up with him anyway."

"So, no boyfriend?"

"No, I don't have a boyfriend."

So he grabbed me again and kissed me like before, only this time I kissed him back.

My time with Colombiano was longer than the last; I had him for two whole weeks—only those two weeks barely felt like two days with all of his games and training sessions. This time was different, we didn't need to start from scratch, so we had more time to see each other for what we really were. We were a couple years older than the last time we had seen each other, making us hopefully a couple more years mature.

Like the last time, we spoke every day but unlike the last time, someone didn't have a secret girlfriend and I sure as hell didn't have a Daddy's Boy. Our two weeks together flew by, and we only had time for one date on, of course, Colombiano's final night. I wanted to make it special, so I took him to my favorite bar where we soaked in a cocktail or two and drank in the live jazz fizzling through the bar. He loved it, like I knew he would, and I loved being the reason for the smile on his face. I drove him back to his hotel, he kissed me goodnight, and we sorrowfully said our goodbyes.

Colombiano left a few days before my twenty-second birthday, and although he was gone, he without a doubt sent me the most heartfelt birthday wishes from thousands of miles away. I didn't care that he was missing my birthday; it wasn't a big deal to me. Besides, I hadn't any real plans except to go shopping with my mom and then later that night I would get "turnt" with two of my friends (my only two friends).

Colombiano and I had discussed before his departure that we would continue speaking, this time I expressed that we had to talk every day otherwise, I would not commit. He assured me that he was committed to me one hundred percent and would come back soon, but that he would love for me to come and meet his entire family in person. In other words, he was shamelessly asking me to go to Colombia after that plan had failed disastrously a couple of years before. I considered it but brushed the idea aside. I was in summer school, and within a week of summer school ending, I would start back up at school. So I had no time to go to Colombia to play lovers in paradise.

While out shopping with my mom, the birthday wishes were flowing like hot cakes through my phone. *I'm like so popular...oh my gawd.*[70] All the while, I was talking to Colombiano about my day and how I wished he was there with me. Then suddenly, the terrible awful happened. An unwanted but much appreciated text came in from Daddy's Boy. He wished me the best on my birthday and said that he had a surprise for me. *A surprise for me? Uhh, hi. We don't talk anymore. Remember? Remember that big, ugly fit you threw? Remember when you called me a liar? I do!*

Apparently my ignoring him didn't register. In the midst of ignoring DB's creepy texts (in which he acted like everything was A-OK), I had decided that I would drop out of the three weeks I had left of summer school and go to Colombia—because when else would I have an opportunity like this to travel? The idea of leaving everything behind was too romantic for me to pass up. My mom agreed, so I sent Colombiano the dates I had in mind, which he responded to enthusiastically. I had one month to plan my wedding—I mean, trip!

Coincidentally during my plans to fly to love, DB sent me a text stating that he had planned a vacation for us for my birthday (I kid you not!). This kid was ridiculous! He seriously thought that he could make me want him again by "buying" me a trip somewhere.[71] *Eww. Stop texting me.* I politely refused and reminded him that we hadn't spoken and then even more politely jogged his memory of how he called me a liar. *Remember that?* Then Daddy's Boy freaked out and called me a liar again, so I said, "That's why I don't want to go on a trip with you." He was pissed! He kept texting me but I didn't care. He could have called me (pardon my French) an effing C. U. Next Tuesday[72] and I wouldn't have responded. He was too stupid—and he wasn't even that hot. I had seen his older brother and knew I was getting the short end

---

[70] Truth be told, only my aunts and cousins and my TWO friends were wishing me happy birthday. I'm not popular.

[71] I call him Daddy's Boy for a reason. He didn't buy me the trip, it was his family vacation and Daddy paid for it and the psycho had told his dad that he was going to bring his "girlfriend."

[72] This is from *Sex and the City*. It means cunt which just so happens to be one of my favorite words. So yes, he could have called me my favorite word and I would have just laughed.

of the gene pool stick. His brother was a babe and a lawyer, and DB was an insurance salesman with an addictive personality and illogical outbursts. *Yeah. No thank you.* I left it like that and I continued to plan for my trip to Medellin, Colombia.

The month leading up to my trip came and went. On September 9, I set out to spend fifteen days in a foreign country all alone, with no one but my lover and his family. I didn't know what to expect. Colombiano and I had spoken every day leading up to this very big day. I came prepared. With me, I brought an array of gifts, handmade and store bought. For his mother I had made a matching bracelet and necklace set; for his brother I had bought a hat and shirt that embodied the "California" lifestyle; for his father I had bought a photography coffee table book (since he himself is a photographer); and for my beloved, I bought a watch that was supposed to represent our patience in time. I had even gotten the damn dog a gift, a bag of wonderfully overpriced dog treats from my favorite bakery, Susie Cakes. I was prepared to dazzle and dazzle them I would.

My plane landed some time around 10 p.m. in the dinky Medellin airport. My stomach sunk as I read the service bars on my phone, "NO SERVICE" and realized I had forgotten to call my carrier to ask them if I had international. *Dooh.* We exited the plane and I tried searching for Wi-Fi. Nothing. My phone wouldn't connect. I tried not to panic but I had never done this before. I had never flown alone thousands of miles away to a country that didn't speak English for a guy that I had seemingly only "met" twice. *Great. What do I do? What if he doesn't remember to come get me? Oh shit, and I can't look at my Facebook for his address! You idiot, why didn't you write that down?!*

I grabbed my bag and trudged through customs. I was so nervous because I didn't know his address and even more scared that they would think I was a drug smuggler (I know, I'm stupid) that when the customs agent asked me in Spanish why I was in the country, I couldn't speak Spanish. *Uhhhhhhh.* He laughed and then repeated himself in English. "Oh!" *Lightbulb. "Por amor,"* I seriously joked with him. He laughed again and then asked me where this love of mine was staying. I froze. I told him I didn't know the address because I was a dummy and I hadn't put it in my phone and the address was saved on my Facebook but I couldn't access it because I didn't have any service. He chuckled again, stamped my passport and let me pass through. *What?*

So I got through customs with absolutely no problem[73] and now I had to face my next problem…NO SERVICE. It was a huge problem that created all of these other smaller problems, like the fact that I couldn't call my beloved to ask if he was on his way to get me or to find his address if he never showed up to get me. *God, what if he never comes to get me?? What should I do?*

I stood in the middle of the airport mulling over my next step, frantically searching for Wi-Fi when I decided to step out of the airport to the pickup area. *Nope, no Colombiano.* I didn't even know what kind of car he drove, so that was a pointless waste of my time. I had no idea what I was doing or where any of this was going and all I wanted to do was cry. I stepped back inside, optimistically thinking that there would be better Wi-Fi indoors. I had my phone out and up to my eye level, taking slow steps in areas that I thought would have a better connection, when this short, five-foot-tall man grabbed my phone from me and started walking around saying lord knows what. He spoke Spanish but I could not understand him for the life of me. All I could think was: *fucking great, now I don't have a phone because this shorty stole it.* He kept saying something and I had no idea what he was trying to tell me, and all I could really focus on was the fact that his grimy little baby hands had my new iPhone 5. He wasn't walking away with my phone but he was scaring the shit out of me. I now had a new BIG problem: I had no phone (which was increasingly bigger than my previous problem of no service).

I began to size this shorty up. *I'm 5'6", so I have at least six inches on this fool. How fast is he? I'm probably faster than him, right? I mean, my legs end at his chest. His legs are like little baby nubs compared to mine so that makes me faster…right? Oh shit, I wonder if he has a whole crew with him. I wonder if this is a setup. What if he's trying to get me to chase him. I need to catch him before it clicks that I'm on to him and his ploy.*

---

[73] This is only because I'm white AF and sounded dumb AF.

Right when I was about to jump this little man for my phone, I heard someone say, "Can I help you?" I looked up to find a man dressed in the airport's uniform.

"Yeah, he took my phone and I don't know what he's saying."

He asked my little sticky fingered friend what he was doing to which he replied that he was trying to fix my phone but the Internet wasn't working...*obviously.* The uniformed man then asked me who I was waiting for, and I told him—cramming his ears with as much detail as I could. He listened to my pathetic story and told me I could use his phone.

I snagged my phone back from the little man as the airport attendant walked me outside to the waiting area and handed me his phone to dial the number. I called the only number I had...no answer. I hung up the phone and looked to my rescuer, who reassured me that they were probably on their way to come and get me. I thought about it and took solace in the idea. I'm not sure how much I bought into it, but for the time being, it would satiate my worries. We stood in silence for a few minutes as the smog from the bustling taxis and busses began to crowd our lungs, and the departing bodies of the airport arrivals flew past us to their appropriate vehicles.

Facebook, it dinged in my head...*I need to message him on Facebook.* I asked to borrow my new friend's phone again and logged into my Facebook. Moments later, his phone lit to life with a message from my beloved; he was almost at the airport. Relief shook through my body as I logged out of my Facebook and handed the phone back to the best airport employee I have ever met.

True to his word, Colombiano arrived at the airport pickup area within ten minutes. With him, and true to Latin men form, he brought his mother. She was breathtakingly beautiful in real life, which kind of intimidated me—No, it scared the shit out of me.

They got out of the car and hugged me as cars honked their horns for him to move out of the way. His mother quickly gathered her purse from the front seat and moved to the back to which I replied, "No." God, that made me feel even more uncomfortable. I had been there

CONCH SHELL CONFESSIONALS

for only a couple of minutes and I was already inconveniencing her.[74]
I pleaded with her to take her front seat back, which she ignored and
carried on contently in the back (this was a great sign for me...it meant
she already liked me). Mama talked most of the forty-five minute drive
home. She filled the car with stereotyped Spanish phrases and motherly
words. It was like a dream to me—I had done it. I had finally made it
to Colombia.

Although cloaked in the dark blanket of night, I could already see
that Colombia was vastly different than the United States. Motorcycles,
cars, and trucks zipped past us as we descended our way into the valley
that was Medellin. I wanted to absorb every moment, every second of this
new place. Lights colored Colombiano's face in greens and reds while his
mama's words began to fade into background noise as the bustling city's
song enrobed my eardrums. Medellin was a cacophonous symphony of
perfection. I was about to have my heart broken again by a lost boy and
fall madly in love with the mother of all mothers—Medellin.

We arrived back at their two-story apartment where I was
enthusiastically greeted by all of the faces I had already met through
Skype—his brother, his father, and their dog. I carefully handed each of
them their gifts and self-consciously watched as each of them unwrapped
their tokens of my gratitude. I was terrified that they weren't going to
like them or that I hadn't gotten them enough for them opening up
their home to me for the next fifteen days. I let out a tiny breath of relief
as each of their faces creased in to smiles at the sight of their gifts. After
all of the excitement blew over, Colombiano led me to his room which
he had been banished from by his mother, but where I was graciously
invited to sleep in for the entirety of my trip, alone. I gathered my
luggage, placed it in my new room, kissed everyone goodnight, laid my
head on Colombiano's pillow and fell into a deep sleep.

The following morning I awoke to a richness of smells and sounds.
I peered out of my foreign bedroom window to see that our house sat

---

[74] Latin Mommy 101: Never piss off the mom...or you'll never be in the family's
good graces. So if you want her son's wiener, you better kiss the floor she walks on
without her knowing you're kissing her ass because then you'll be a kiss ass, and no
one likes those.

high above the ramshackle rooftops of its neighbors. In the distance, I could see the outline of the mountains that surrounded the City of Eternal Spring and almost close enough to touch were the cascading clouds that were about to bring us a bounty of rain. I stripped myself of my sleep-ridden pajamas and carefully dressed for a day to remember.

The day started normally enough with a typical Colombian breakfast. I sat at the glass table with my beloved to my left, his brother to my right, his mother across from me and their dog at my feet. My setting was adorned with fresh, homemade juice, coffee, eggs, *arepas* (they're like a thick tortilla...only a million times better), butter, and *galletas* (crackers). I indulged my selfish belly as Colombiano and Mama went over the plans for my day. I didn't have to lift a finger (although I tried). Our breakfast table was lively, a culmination of familiarity mixed with the excitement of unfamiliarity. This and only a few more mornings following this first day would be so lively.

On my third day, I discovered that Colombiano was still speaking to his "ex" girlfriend. (Yes, the same girl from the last time.) I wasn't trying to snoop or catch him in a lie. In fact, I hadn't suspected anything until one morning I walked upstairs to their office to ask him if we had any plans for that day. Upon hearing my voice, he slammed his laptop shut and turned his chair to face me as a guilty, lying man. I had caught him on Facebook messenger talking to her but ignored his obvious guilt and carried on normally as to avoid causing drama in my foreign home.

As each day passed, he grew more distant and most of my time was spent with his mother who had a growing obsession with my hair, since I had what she called, "*efrizz*."[75] So most of my time was spent with Mama and virtually only her. Colombiano had come up with the excuse that he was too busy with work and so stressed for his upcoming championship water polo game, which was the fourth day of my trip. But just the week before when we had been thousands of miles apart, he had filled my head with ideas of traveling to the neighboring towns, and just weeks before that he had sung with the endless possibilities of adventure. Now days into my trip, he was dry with regret and treachery.

---

[75] That's Spanish for frizz.

I had given him the benefit of the doubt. So desperately I wanted to ignore the truth that I knew I was facing and so desperately I tried. I thought that maybe he was really distracted by work and that the stress of his big game was weighing heavy on him. I didn't know what to do except to take his word and hope for the best. Besides, I couldn't fathom him denying and lying to me a second time. (In hindsight, I just didn't want it to be true.) So I carried out my trip as planned.

On the fourth day, my betraying beloved played in the national championship. From the stands high above the pool, I prayed to the high heavens that they would win. I needed them to win. I needed him to be normal. I wanted him to be normal. I wanted him to be the man he was before, the man that had come back to California to tell me that he wanted to be with me. The man that had told me on the spot that he loved me and thought about me every day that I hadn't spoken to him. The same man that asked for forgiveness for his sins against me. I wanted him to love me the way that I (thought I) loved him.

Someone up there wanted to shut my bellyaching up, so Colombiano's team won the championship. I was ecstatic. He was ecstatic. The team was ecstatic. The game ended, the crowd cheered and the men of the team planned for a night on the town. Mama forced Colombiano to take me with him.[76] She was probably the most excited for our night out on the town. In fact, she took it as an opportunity to subtly suggest that I fix my "*efrizz*." Honestly, this was probably the only reason she was so happy. She came barreling into my room as I was getting ready and laid out an armful of hair products on my bed—gel, mouse, hairspray, and various oils. I guess my frizzy hair was bothering her. I ignored her products and braided my processed, frizzy hair.

Even with my hair less frizzy, Colombiano wasn't exactly Mr. Happy with his blonde American "girlfriend" by his side…he was pissed. He was so bothered that I was with him, I kept trying to talk to him, and he would shut me down. He had that look on his face as though he had somewhere better to be with someone better than me. (He didn't.) We went to dinner just the two of us in *Parque Lleras* (which is Medellin's

---

[76] Yes, I'm being dead serious…she forced him.

hip and happening area…tons of bars and tons of fun). Colombiano decided for the both of us that we would eat Cuban food and then meet up with the guys from his team a little later. He and dinner were awful, but we had the rest of the night to hopefully make things better. I had prayed for him to be happier after winning his game and instead he was more irritable than before.

We finished our awful dinner and started walking toward the bar where we were meeting everyone else. Colombiano stopped me before we walked inside and told me that we had to buy our drinks at the store down the street since this bar didn't sell non-alcoholic beer. (I should've known here that he wasn't going to stop being a bitch toward me… non-alcoholic beer?) I didn't question him, I just followed his lead and went with him to the store. *He better not think that I'm drinking that piss water.* He paid for his golden not real beer, and we headed back to the bar.

I was kind of getting to that point where my brain likes to say, *I don't give a fuck and I'm going to do what I want,* so I marched back into the bar and bought myself a real beer.[77] Colombiano rudely headed up the stairs where everyone else was without waiting for me. *Asshole.*

The men and their girls were circled up around a tiny table atop the untrustworthy-looking floor planks of the second story. Dead center on the little table was a carton of *Aguardiente,* a liquor native to Colombia that tastes like black licorice. I sat down on the plastic stool next to my beloved piece of shit, and the men enthusiastically greeted me, pouring me a dixie cup shot of the clear liquor. *Mmmm, not bad.* Then they poured me another. *Salud to you.* And then another. *This is not alcohol; there's no burn to it.* Colombiano was ignoring me, but the rest of the team was loving me. He wouldn't introduce me to any of the other girlfriends, and when it came time to dance, he said he didn't dance… *You're Colombian, you idiot, you dance.* So I asked "Esteven" to hit the floor and he danced with me.

Like the bodies of our makeshift dance floor, the sketchy wooden planks rattled with every bass beat of the blasting music. The shots were

---

[77] Dead serious…beer fucks me up.

pouring, the bodies were grinding, and I was finally having fun. Stupid Colombiano sat on his plastic chair and acted like he was too good to pay attention to me, that is until...

Everyone in our party was up and dancing. Girls and guys were all over the place—only there were more men than women. Some of the men were trying to be generous to the other guys that didn't have a girl to dance with, so they began hoisting up some of the girls onto the tiny tables to dance for everyone. I tried to hide in the corner, knowing that my beloved would despise me making a drunken spectacle of myself. Honest to god, I tried. I failed, but hey! I'm not judging myself.

All of the sudden I was lifted from my dark corner and placed smack dab in the middle of our dance floor atop of a tiny plastic table. Colombiano looked up...I froze...then I did the only thing I knew how to do...I twerked. The crowd went crazy, and Colombiano looked like he was about to go crazy (as in angry...not turned on or the slightest bit amused). I didn't care anymore. The guys lifted me off of the table, and some girls came up to me and asked me how I learned to dance like that. *Oh, Alcohol taught me.* I kept dancing, not going anywhere near Colombiano. Finally, he got up from his shit-throne-of-a-plastic-stool and started dancing with another girl. I didn't care; I was dancing with someone way hotter.

Suddenly, my dance partner swung me back, picked me up and I was hoisted back onto the table to dance again. *Oops, I did it again.* This time, Colombiano was so pissed at me that he walked away from his lovely new dance partner and shortly after I came off of the table, he pulled me away and told me it was time to go. *Muhahaha, did I do that?*

The whole fifteen-minute ride home I got an earful from Colombiano about how rude I was and how I made a fool of myself and how all of his friends would think he was like that[78] and that's why he doesn't drink because he doesn't need to be crazy and blah, blah, blah.

I will admit that I was drunk, but drunk or not, I didn't want to hear the shit that was spewing out of his mouth. I mean, this is the same guy that invited me to his country to meet his family and his friends

---

[78] Note: If they're really your friends, then who the fuck cares?

because he wanted to spend time with me, and now here I was, only he didn't want to get to know me. He wanted to ignore me and talk to his "ex" girlfriend. I had had enough. I exploded, erupting in tears and anger with all of his empty promises and how I had seen who he was talking to the day before and how I went there for HIM. Colombiano shut up, and we drove the rest of the way home in silence—no sorries and definitely no kisses goodnight. I thought that he just needed time to digest my truthful words. I was wrong.

Nothing changed after that night. Everything remained the same, and to a degree, it got worse. Colombiano wouldn't talk to me, he wouldn't give me the time of day. We ate breakfast together with the entire family and then, he would go off to "work" which meant he was on Facebook looking at other girls' profiles while talking to the "ex." *Whatever.* At least I had his mom. Seriously though, she taught me so much about Colombia. She and I spent every day together. We would run errands and get coffee and stop and talk to complete strangers. She was such a phenomenal woman, and she made me feel like I had someone when everyone felt so far away. Mama was my saving grace on this trip. In fact, she is the reason that I can look back on this otherwise awful trip with such fondness.

My fifteen days in Medellin were coming to an end and on my final full day there, I decided that if I didn't do "it" then, then I would always regret it. So I did "it," I asked Colombiano while we sat outside of his apartment building waiting for his mom, "Don't you want to kiss me?"

He laughed and leaned his car seat back, "No, you're so funny." I was confused by his answer because weeks before he couldn't shut up about how he wouldn't be able to stop kissing me once I got to Medellin.

"So you don't want to kiss me?" I asked confusedly.

"I don't want to spend the rest of my life with you." *Oh. I don't think that's what I asked. Also, that was really mean.* "But I want you to be my friend forever," he added as I remained silent.

Just then, his mom got into the car. That coy son of a gun acted like nothing was wrong and like we had an amazing day, but obviously, he was just thinking of his day and himself. I had been told that I never had a chance with the guy that I still felt wanted to be with me even after the lack of attention and absence of kisses. I wasn't sure if I was going to cry or punch him. The whole ride to the grocery store, he kept trying to engage me in his pointless conversation to hide his lying, cheating ways from his mother. *Bastard. I hope your "ex" gives you infinite blue balls and that your balls explode from all of your angry sperm.*

Colombiano dropped his mother and me off at the grocery store while he drove away to water polo practice. As I exited the car, he grabbed my hand and leaned in as if he was going to kiss me. My heart dropped, and steam smoked out of my ears as I looked at him, considered punching him square in the nose but came to my senses and turned away. It was my final night in Medellin, and his mother wanted to make sure I had enough supplies for my trip back home, and Colombiano wanted to make sure he looked good in front of his mother.

I was so upset. Mama kept talking and talking as we walked through the aisles, only I wasn't listening (which was unusual) and eventually, she figured out something was wrong. When she asked me, I was too embarrassed to tell her the truth, so I lied and said that I was tired—but she knew it was a lie and asked me again.

After some hesitation, I told her what had happened, I told her everything—how I had known Colombiano was still talking to his ex, how he had ignored me for most of the trip, how I asked him why he wouldn't kiss me anymore and how he seemed to have just changed his mind overnight. Her jaw dropped in confusion. Mama hadn't noticed the distance or anything else I had confided in her. I was nearly in tears as I revealed to her all of my newly discovered findings and feelings. She grabbed my hand and told me how upset she was with him and that tomorrow she would sit down and ask him why. I looked at this magnificently beautiful women whom I had called *suegra*[79] for the duration of my trip, with an ocean of tears brimming in my eyes, and I asked her not to mention any of this to her son. We finished our grocery shopping, grabbed a cup of coffee and went back home.

When we got home, Colombiano acted like nothing was wrong, like he hadn't just crushed my heart and fed it to the wolves. I was not

---

[79] Mother of my significant other

playing games, and I was intolerant of any of his bullshit. My head was spinning as I secretly planned to leave in the dead of the morning alone, I didn't need that lying philanderer to drive me to the airport. I could do it all by my lonesome, man-hating self.

Colombiano interrupted my thoughts, corralling me in his arms. I broke away. He shot a snarky remark at me as to show me who was the man. *No, I'll show you who wears the pants around here now.* I shot him down. No smirk, no just kidding, no emotion—just shot down. He stood slack-jawed in the kitchen. "Goodnight," I said to cut the dagger deeper as I walked to his room. I shut the door, and I cried. I cried out all of my frustrations and broken fantasies on his bed, that bed of broken dreams. I heard him walk up to the door and listen for me. I silenced myself and fell asleep.

The next morning I was shaken awake by him. It was 4:30 a.m. and apparently I hadn't woken up early enough to avoid him. He greeted me with a shitty tasting cup of coffee and grin that said he was still a little boy. I rolled my bag out of his room, left a note on the kitchen table and hugged his parents goodbye. It was bittersweet knowing how much I loved his family but knowing that I would probably never see them again. We drove the nearly forty-five-minute drive to the airport in silence, me, Colombiano and his brother. I only broke my self-proclaimed speechlessness to speak to his brother and would blatantly ignore Colombiano when he spoke to me. (Yeah, I know…so mature.)

We arrived at the airport, and I grabbed my things to trek onward alone but was stopped by his brother when he grabbed my bag from me and walked into the check-in area with me while Colombiano trailed behind us. His wonderful brother captured me in a tight hug and whispered to me how much he would miss me. I hugged him tighter as I tried to fight the tears—I loved that kid. Then I walked to Colombiano to say goodbye and give him a hug that says "We're acquaintances" but was instead met with a kiss. That motherfucking bastard planted a fat kiss on my lips to say goodbye. I smacked him in the face, "What was that for?"

"Because I felt like it," he smirked.

I gathered my bags and trudged to the check-in line, as I looked back I could see both boys smiling and waving. I moved up in line and turned to find them again but could only see their backs as they ducked into their car.

My whole plane ride back to Miami, my lips screamed with Colombiano's kiss. It was death. His kiss was death. My entire trip I had begged for him to kiss me and love me, and then finally he did it when it was too late. I was so confused. I couldn't stop thinking about it. I was angry but a hopelessly simpleminded romantic. That kiss screwed with my head for the entirety of my fifteen-hour flight back home and the couple of weeks following my return. There I was, this stupidly naive twenty-two-year-old girl who had convinced herself that she was in love and followed this "love" to a country thousands of miles away.

Colombiano didn't love me, he loved the idea of me—and I never loved him, I loved the idea of him. We had both been selfishly "in love" with the other. We loved for all of the wrong reasons, but at the time I hadn't a clue of any of this. I was dead set on this "love." I wracked my brain with every empty moment we had. *Why didn't he try to hold my hand at the movies? Why didn't he kiss me when we used to kiss? Why did he kiss me at the airport? Why didn't he want to take me anywhere? Why wouldn't he look at me?* My insecurities were imploring me to insanity. I didn't know what to do. That kiss was death, and that death was temporary insanity. Colombiano was gone. We would never be, but I couldn't wrap my psychotically starry-eyed head around that. I needed a wake-up call, and it would come to me in the form of a weird-ass dream.

●● ● ●●

ELEPHAS MAXIMUS INDICUS[80]

●● ● ●●

It came to me in a dream.

●● ● ●●

Censorship has never been so real and since someone, somewhere is telling me what I can't do, then let me tell you what you can do: visit www.daxmarie.com to read this oh-so forbidden chapter. I'm not political but, apparently, I'm controversial.

---

[80] That's science talk for an Indian elephant.

BLACK AS NIGHT (A.K.A. HOT MESS)

Remember when I puked on that date?

A few short weeks after my elephant dream that I am not allowed to mention, I decided to follow through on the new "challenge" I had posed to myself. After deciphering the perverse nature of my dream, I concluded that I needed to be a "yes" woman, meaning that whoever asked me for my phone number and on a date, I would have to say yes. The whole point of this "challenge" was to get me out of my comfort zone of school, work, and the tiny exclusive group of friends I had (by which I mean two. I had and still have only two friends). But mostly, I wanted this to be a platform for me to be less judgmental with men and, more importantly, myself.

See, up until this point in my life, I hadn't had the best experiences with guys (I am not blaming all of this on guys, I take one hundred percent responsibility for my stupid actions and choices). I thought that by being a "yes" woman, I would understand there was more to a relationship than the physicality and superficiality of what I thought it meant to be in a relationship and in love. So I challenged myself, wanting to charge through my self-inflicted obstacles and hatch some new experiences and memories. Well, I definitely spawned some raunchy memories and disgusting realizations when I initiated my "yes" woman challenge.

Say this in an announcer's voice: "And in this corner, our first contender. All the way from the hard streets of upper-middle-class

93

Philly, standing in at five feet, five inches, we have Poor Schmuck."
[The crowd goes wild.]

Have you guys met yet? Well, let me introduce him to you…Poor
Schmuck, meet everyone. Everyone, meet Poor Schmuck. I will tell you
right now: this man was wonderfully sweet. He brought me my earrings
even after I blacked-out and puked in his car.[81] Just recently, he sent me
the picture that he took of me while I was barfing out of his car…Isn't
that so sweet?! (Okay, that was maybe a little creepy of him.) Ladies, he's
still single and comes from a respectable Jewish family, so if you want
him, I'm sure I could set something up.

Back to my challenge. So it had been some time since my dream
and since I had inflicted this game on myself. I was still working at
the same uppity restaurant, only now I was waiting tables in the bar,
which meant more money and more time to mingle with the guests. It
was a Friday night in November, and the restaurant was starting to die
down. My tables were nearly empty except for a few couples trickled
throughout who kept to themselves. Suddenly a vociferous group of
four men drunkenly frisked their way to one of my tables. I could tell
that they were already a little (just a little) inebriated and that they were
going to be a blast and be fatty-style tippers if I flirted with them. *Oh
yeah, bring it on baby!*

So I approached the table, giving them my usual introductory
words and was immediately met with saucy replies, so I got a bit spicy
in return. They were eating up my sassiness and I was swallowing whole
their attention. The party of four ordered some drinks and continued to
egg me on as I badgered them. An hour or so passed and it was time to
close, "Fellas, I hate to do this to you, but we're doing last call. Is there
anything else I can get you?"

"Yeah, what's your phone number?!" one of them jested.

Seeing the game we were all playing, I shot out my seven-digit
phone number as quickly as I could—"Is that nine-four-nine area
code?" another one said.

---

[81] It was outside of his car, but I was still seat belted into the car when I was spewing
my guts out.

CONCH SHELL CONFESSIONALS

"Why yes, I believe it is," I facetiously fired back.

They closed out their tab with me and merrily left the restaurant.

The following afternoon I received a text from Poor Schmuck. I hadn't even noticed him taking my number down. Apparently, he had memorized my digits. His message said what a pleasure it was to meet me and how he would love to take me on a date that week. I knew exactly who he was, given the self-deprecating tone in the text, in which he questioned if I even remembered who he was. *Uh, hi, you were the drunk one remember? Not me. I just served you the alcohol.* In accordance to my challenge, I agreed, and we set a date a few days out.

Poor Schmuck had picked this new gastropub ten minutes from my home. He set the time for 8:00 p.m., giving me enough time to get back to Orange County from L.A. with a decent amount of time to change and get ready for our date. I rushed out of class and onto the freeway, got home and dressed, and headed out to meet him. I arrived at the pub about fifteen minutes early. I thought I would've gotten there much earlier than PS since he had work, but I was wrong. When I got there, I scanned the bar and saw him sitting at the corner table of the bar with his back to the door. I steadied myself as I approached and saw that Poor Schmuck had already ordered himself a drink and some food (a little rude, but whatever). His face was red and sprinkled with sweat…he was nervous, but so was I.

The hours passed and again, we found ourselves at closing time. Conversation had been nonstop, talking about everything from our youth up until the moment we were spending together. I came to find out that Poor Schmuck was twelve years my senior, which didn't scare me but surprised him when he found out how young I was. There weren't any lulls in conversation or any awkward moments until, we stood up to leave. Upon standing, I realized just how much shorter Poor Schmuck was compared to me (which was about three inches in the booties I was wearing), not to mention how drunk he was—he had three glasses of wine with me, as well as one before my arrival. I was buzzed, and he was hammered drunk.

We walked outside together, I to my car and him to wait for his Uber. PS seemed tiny to me. I hadn't seen him stand up before, even when I served his table, he was seated the entire time, and when they left, I had gone to the kitchen. So I never saw him in all of his sky-scraping glory, and it made me uncomfortable. We kept talking while I waited with him for his Uber then, he did it—he leaned in to kiss me and, quickly, I darted back. I was embracing my new "non" judgmental challenge, but I still was too judgmental to let a man shorter than I kiss me.

So, I may have been too shallow for a kiss but not too shallow to accept a second date with him. I gladly accepted once he recuperated himself from my jumping back denial and abruptly said, "I would love to take you out again." I liked his confidence, and we had a phenomenal conversation the whole night. I didn't see any harm in accepting another date, in fact, I figured that dating and letting someone kiss me again would be something that I had to ease into. So with graceless ease, I faced my new challenge.

Some weeks passed before our second date. Poor Schmuck was busy traveling for work, and I was busy with school, so I didn't mind the gap in our dates. D-Day was finally upon us, and I was a crashing calamity not to be messed with. Poor Schmuck set our date for some club in Hollywood where he had gotten us into V.I.P. since his friend was the club's music producer. He wanted to pick me up from my house in Orange County. I tried to convince him that it would be better if we met in Hollywood since I was already in L.A. for the entire day and didn't want to sit in rush hour traffic to get back home only to have to turn back around.

For some reason, it didn't click in PS's brain that it would have been a million times easier for me to meet him there. So, instead, I rushed home with only forty minutes to shower, do my makeup and get dressed for a club. (Ladies, I think we can all attest to the fact that it is better to take your time with winged eyeliner.)

I had made it home, brawling my way through rush hour traffic with a whole forty minutes to spare. Now it was time to rush through touching up my hair and slapping on a full face of makeup. *God, this is going to be so fun!* Hopping in the shower, I nearly slipped flat on my back; re-curling my hair, resulted in a hapless wave; but the cherry-topper being when I stabbed myself in the eyeball as I stroked my lashes long with mascara. *Great!* I had nearly killed myself getting ready for a date that I wasn't all too sure I wanted to go on, but I had made it. I did it…and I soon lost it.

I hadn't any time left to spare when PS sent me a text that stated he was running late. *You bastard! DO YOU KNOW WHAT I JUST WENT THROUGH?!* It was already 7:37 p.m. and he was already late. Initially, it was just a ten minutes "late," but what he actually meant was twenty-four minutes…only twenty-four. I was infuriated![82]

I waited. And waited. And waited. I could feel my blood boiling and skin itching with anxiety as each second tick-tocked by. I needed to relax. I was going completely against my challenge's motive, so I grabbed the bottle of tequila my friend, Rambo, had brought me from Mexico, and I poured myself a decent but not overly zealous-sized shot to sip on. The burn on my lips was exactly what I needed to distract myself from the hunger in my belly[83] and the irritability in my brain.

With a nice buzz buzzing through my being, Poor Schmuck texted me stating that he was lost. (Obviously, he, didn't listen to me when I told him to call me when he got to my neighborhood since the GPS never takes people to my house.) As a changed and civilized character, I called him to direct him to my whereabouts. Apparently, chivalry was dead because he decided it best to keep his car far out on the street and make me walk to him. *Lovely.*[84] I grabbed my purse and hiked my high-heeled ass to his very far car.

When I finally reached his car, I tried to maintain composure in my tight boa constrictor dress. He didn't get out to open my door or even open it from the driver's side. Instead, he sat back and watched as I struggled to duck into his low-sitting car with my five-inch heels. I gathered myself and glanced over to say hello and—what the?! PS was not dressed for a club!

---

[82] You always know when you're not going to be on time and you should share this VITAL info with the person waiting for your late ass.

[83] I thought he was taking me to dinner since he was picking me up at dinner time…

[84] I expect door-to-door service on a date, as should every woman.

He shifted the car into drive and I exclaimed, "Wait, I think I should change. I'm way overdressed."

"No you're perfect," he assured me.

"You're dressed very casually, and I think I'm way too dressed up," I complained unconvinced.

"I always dress like this and I told you to dress like that. You look fantastic." He winked.

Compliments or not, I was not happy that I was dressed up nicely and he was dressed for a damn backyard barbecue. That 5'5" squirrel had told me to "wear a sexy dress and heels." *Great, Elizabeth and James meet Kmart men's department.*

He continued shifting the car into drive and out of my neighborhood. My buzz was gone halfway through our long and perilous journey on the freeway because he drove like an old man. He wouldn't get into the freakin' carpool lane and I was dying inside, it was taking every microscopic molecule of my being to not be a backseat driver. *DYING* I tell you!

Finally, we arrived at the club. We exited the car, I at a whopping 5'11" and my compadre at a meager 5'5." We were a sight for sore eyes (or maybe we made eyes sore?). *Don't be shallow.* Entering the club, I felt my annoyance grow as I critiqued PS's outfit for one last, sober time—faded blue jeans, a balled-up, ashy blue cotton t-shirt and ratchet running shoes. *You're being a bitch. Just have fun.*

We were so early and I was so hungry! He shooed me to the bar to take advantage of our unlimited drinks before 9:00. Avion Tequila was sponsoring the event...*Ooh, maybe this won't be so bad.* I took mine on the rocks as a means to slow my roll, while PS got his mixed with soda water. (Soda water makes me gag. It's too housewifey.) We gallantly sipped on our drinks as he gave me the backstory of his friends before they arrived.

The clock struck nine as Poor Schmuck ordered us our second round and it was with drinks in hand that we met his friend and his girlfriend. The two couples, we chatted a bit. I was getting to know them, and they were getting to know me. I was two drinks in, and I didn't even feel a buzz which was strange for me, considering I wasn't exactly (and still am not) the strongest drinker. The music started pumping as we finished our second round of drinks and glided our way toward V.I.P. Nothing—I felt nothing—not even the slightest bit mind altered. Alas, my schmuck returned with drinks as did my annoyance with him. *Ruh-roh.*

The beat was banging and I was growing restless. Apparently, two and a half drinks (not including the one I drank at home) were now pumping through my bloodstream with every palpitation of the electronic music set. Poor Schmuck had returned with our third round of drinks and instead of enjoying it with me, he decided it more fun to network. *Uh, hi, yeah…remember me?…The giant? Yeah, hi there, lil' guy, I'm ready to dance now.* I couldn't take it anymore! I wanted to move my body and he was too busy business-ing it up with some other bore. *Why are you networking at a time like this?* My irritation grew…I wanted to dance. No, I needed to dance!

So, I self-medicated with another sip of tequila and let the beat of the bass boogie through me. At first, my dance moves were subtle and so sexy.[85] There I was, dancing all alone like a princess locked in her high tower. I was trapped in V.I.P. with no one to entertain me. (Oh, poor me.) I looked out over the dance floor, staring at all of the other dancing schmucks who weren't in V.I.P. and then over to my Poor Schmuck who wouldn't dance.

I was really starting to get into it. With PS (who was paying no mind to me) to my left and a whole bobbing dance floor in front of me, I began to let loose. I held onto the railing with one hand for stability, and with my other, I carefully clutched my watered down tequila. I was dancing away. Calm, cool, and so sexy (nope, still not sexy), but suddenly my feet began to slide outwards away from each other like two magnets repelling each other apart. *Whoa, I'm slipping. Nah, I've got this. No one will even* notice.

Have you ever seen a baby giraffe learning to walk? Yeahhhh, that's what I looked like, all knobby kneed with my feet sliding outwards

---

[85] Note: Drunk dancing is never sexy but this is my story so, for my sake please just let me be sexy.

and my body sinking downwards. Eventually, I dropped so low that I was as short as Poor Schmuck, and when he realized, he leveraged his arm under mine and propped me back up. *Whoops.* I was mortified, and the worst part was that he didn't even turn away from his other conversation. He just pulled me back up like a dad does to a little kid without missing a beat. *So rude.*

I sat for a second or two twiddling my thumbs in my brain (because at this point, I was too drunk to physically do this) and then it hit me: *I have legs...I can walk away.* Upon this realization and even after my baby giraffe legs incident, I still hadn't a clue that I was drunk. I began to scan V.I.P. since I thought it too much work to walk down the stairs to the dance floor. Then BAM, I saw my next mission to self-entertainment.

I had noticed this guy earlier and not because he was good looking but because he had been on his phone the entire night. He had been sitting on his couch all alone with his eyes fixated on his tiny phone screen, even with the electronic music blasting. I didn't get it, and it had been annoying me that he wasn't giving the DJ the time of day to appreciate his music that I obviously enjoyed so much. (I was a huge patron of the arts that night.)[86] So, I tapped PS on the shoulder, shoved my water mess of a drink into his hand, and sauced my way over to the couch to give this guy a piece of my mind.

Plopping myself on the couch next to him, I interrupted with: "YOu's bE ON ta phon AAA niGHt," which translates to: you've been on your phone all night.

"Ahh I'm sorry. Here, let me get off of that for you."

Whoops, I thought, when I drunkenly realized that he probably thought I was hitting on him. "Uh, yuh," I said triggering my index finger and thumb at him like an Italian mobster as I tried to stand up to make a quick and clean exit. I failed.

I stood up only to immediately fall backwards onto the couch with my legs rainbowing over my head. I propped myself back up to a sitting position, looked back at the victim of my self-entertainment ploy.

---

[86] I mean, drunk. I was drunk.

"Oopsie," I shrugged at him and stood up without stopping to see his reaction as I walked the four steps back to PS who was exactly where I had left him. I grabbed my drink from his baby hands and, like before, he didn't miss a beat in his conversation as he handed it over to me.

Things began to die down in the club as did Poor Schmuck's business opportunity. He broke away from his conversation to tell me it was time to go. I agreed and we walked toward the exit. He stopped me in front of the bathrooms, "Do you want to use the bathroom before we head back on the road?" I pondered the thought like a little girl and decided that he, the adult was right. *I should use the facilities before we leave.*[87]

We parted ways into our respective bathrooms. Struggling like a fat lush in my tight dress, I tried to lift it over my big ass without ripping the seam. I could hear the stitching crackling as I shimmied it up.[88] Somehow (but thankfully), I managed to slip it up and release all of the tequila from my very full bladder. I washed my hands; checked myself in the mirror, squinting to make my reflection sit still and met up with PS at the door.

Poor Schmuck grabbed my Sasquatch-sized hands with his little kitten paws and led me outside. All I remember was being irritated that he was holding my hand and being even more annoyed when he said, "Let me know if you need me to pull over." He was just being a considerate gentleman, but all I could think was: *Bitch, you obviously don't know me. I've only blacked-out and puked once.* (Since then it's been too many times to count.) I remained silent as he sat me in my seat and buckled me into my carseat and slammed the door shut. The last thing I remember was telling myself not to fall asleep. Then I fell asleep.

To spare you the boredom of telling my complete puke story, I will tell you that I puked. I puked multiple times on the freeway (not sure how many) and once on the way up the hill to my house. It was as simple as PS saying, "We're almost home."

---

[87] My drunk thoughts were more along the lines of: *I go pee.*

[88] I always rip my pants/dresses on the ass seam when I'm drunk...happens nearly every time. Yes, I am an inept child.

And it was as complicated as as me slurring, "Puuuuullll. ov. ov. overrrr."

"Are you sure?" he stammered.

"Bllll. blll. bleggggg." I promptly reassured him with my dry heaving.[89]

Less than a mile, that was the distance to my house where I painted the asphalt with speckled bits of kale chips and añejo tequila. My sloshing stomach acid was at a putrid adhesion to the asphalt while I remained seat belted into PS's car. I evacuated the remaining contents of my stomach and shut my door and then he carried on.

He pulled up to my house, woke me up again to tell me that I was home and let me out of the car without walking a very drunk me to my door. Somehow, I made it the thirty feet to my door and began to fumble through my teeny-tiny purse for my house key. *Ahhh ha!* I found it and with shaking hands, struggled to insert the key into the lock. *Got ya.* I swung the door open, thudding it into the wall and dropping the keys onto the echoing wood floor. Bending over, I attempted to fish up my keys from the floor, "Gaa dam NIT, stoo ped KkkEyss." With ass to the air, I finally managed to hook them with my fingers. Leaving the front door open (my mom told me this the next morning), I tossed them onto the kitchen counter and clanked my heels up the wooden staircase.

Once I reached the top, I unzipped my dress nearly tackling myself to the ground to get the damn thing off. I struggled so hard. But of course, the struggle became much more real when I got myself stuck— both arms tied to my torso because they were caught in the armholes. I wiggled, and I waggled, but I was most definitely stuck.

My mom must have heard all of the commotion and came ripping out of her bedroom, "What's wrong?" she panicked.

I stopped and looked at her with my arms in a tangled mess, "I Maa suchA ba-d. Person."

---

[89] I was going to put the pic of me puking my guts out of Poor Schmuck's car (since he was nice/creepy enough to take one of me) but then my publisher said I would need to get permission for that…so you can go on to my website for the Infamous Puke Pic.

"What? What happened?" She panicked. I wouldn't look at her, all of my remaining brain cells were transfixed by the fact that I was trapped by my dress. "DAX," she screamed as she walked toward me to release me from the clutches of Elizabeth and James. "Dax. What. Happened," she pleaded once more.

"I NA jusss so DrUNk."

Mama stopped mid-stride, did an about-face and went back into her room, "Goodnight." She slammed her door shut and left me in the middle of the hallway, bamboozled by my very tight dress. I struggled a bit longer but somehow, managed to slip it off without ripping it. (There is a God.) The next morning I awoke in backwards pajama pants and a bra and I felt like shit.

What a nightmare I must have been for Poor Schmuck?! He had graciously taken me on a cool date and I gracelessly puked my way home. I felt awful, both physically/mentally. Not to mention how horrible I felt for doing that to him. I had done one of the most disrespectful things I could imagine to a great guy. I didn't know what to do, I was still drunk when I woke up but even through the remnants of my inebriation, I knew that I wasn't ready to date anyone.

Poor Schmuck deserved a woman that was sure of herself, not a girl who was heartbroken over some fantasy of a man she had made up in her head. The same girl (um, me) who had challenged herself to make herself go out on a date. I was pathetic and so embarrassed. Letting my drunken state pass into the most horrible hangover of my life, I texted him later that day and told him the truth—that I didn't think I was ready just yet to date. My hangover lasted me all the way through Monday, when he had only lasted me two dates, trying for a third.[90] I needed some time to grow up.

---

[90] Yes, even after that mess he still asked me on a third date. I politely refused.

∘∘◉∘∘

Soul Searched

∘∘◉∘∘

"The ocean is like a washing machine for my soul."

∘∘◉∘∘

I had given up on romance since I had challenged myself with Poor Schmuck. I didn't want to date, but I had made myself do it. Since Colombia, I hadn't felt like my normal horn-dog self. The trip left me so inspired yet so confused, so much so that I didn't want to date anyone. Without a doubt, Colombiano had made me grow up a little bit and matured my vision of what was real and what was a fantasy inside my head. I had been left with a world of questions—Questions that I hadn't even formulated into questions yet, but I could feel them titillating in the creases of my brain. I had been provoked to ponder the mountain of life and love. I am not saying that my trip and the Colombian ruined love or men for me. All I am saying is they blew out a candle and ignited a fire. I no longer felt sad or angry for the "love" lost.

It was something novel, a way I had never felt before. I guess, in some sense, I felt more connected to me than I had ever felt in my young life. I felt like I was strongly *me*, like I was a complete version of myself, and that had brought with it some new realizations about the life that I had lived and the "loves" I had lost and found.

I began to debate what love was. What was love between a man and a woman? I understood the love between a parent and a child, aunts, cousins, uncles, and friends. But what was love in a romantic relationship? When you're young, and you see two people, a man and a woman, a woman and a woman, or a man and a man, you don't stop to ponder, what is love? You just see them, and it makes sense: they just love each other. But as more years passed and even more men passed through my life, I was wrinkled with the realization that they don't just love each other, so much more goes into the conclusion of love in a relationship. The concept of soulmates absolutely baffled my mind.

In the past, with every guy I dated I thought I had found my soulmate (but the reality of it was that I hadn't a clue of what soulmate meant). When I was ready to start dating again, this thought process of "finding my soulmate" hadn't changed. I thought it was a no-brainer: when I found someone who seemed to be perfect for me, I thought that we would be soulmates.

Until this "soulmate" of mine had to go and mess it all up by "giving" me chlamydia. *What?*

Let me explain. Enter Bun Boy—salt-encrusted shoulder-length hair, a faded pink streak peeking out just underneath the sun-bleached ones, body cut like that of a surfer and mellow vibes for days. He was everything I was not searching for, and I just so happened to stumble upon him. They say that's how true love is found: unsolicited. We'll see about that.

Enter me—hopeless creature of habit, finals week, writing an infinite number of final papers, and caffeinated the fug out as a means to drown out the pain of stamping fingertips against the soulless keyboard of my laptop. I inhabited my usual coffee shop, parking my *derrière* in one of the booths for a couple of hours, downing a medium nonfat caramel latte (with three shots of espresso) and then downsizing my typical americano to a small (two shots of espresso). I was wired, or as Bun Boy liked to say, "on a hot one."

Lub dub, Lub dub—each heartbeat pounded the hypnotic caffeine through my veins, steaming life through my soul and pulsating hypothetical words from my mind to the bright laptop screen. Shit, I was on a hot one. I couldn't stand it any longer. I had to leave. That caffeinated energy could not be contained for another millisecond, and I knew where it could be well spent: SHOPPING. So, with cracked-out hands, I gathered my things and jammed the hell out of there.

Well, it wasn't but a mere hour later that my caffeine binge took a turn for the worst—of course, while I was in the middle of shopping.

Damn it. I had to eat. When I get like this, it is vital to the survival of mankind that I nourish my crackhead body with real food…not that pastry shit I love so much. It is *VITAL*, I tell you.

But solving my problem wasn't as easy as grabbing a bag of chips from a vending machine. I am a creature of habit and there are only a few places where I will eat, and, to make matters even worse, I also believe I can feel the energies of everyone and everywhere when I am caffeinated the fug out. In other words…I become a moody bitch. So I hurriedly walked over to my first choice in an eatery, Pain du Monde. Walked in and walked right back out. I didn't like the "energy" of the restaurant that day, which really meant that I didn't like the snot-faced grimace of the girl sitting in the restaurant. So I ran the other way to mend my insanity with food at the other French restaurant nearby, Le Pain Quotidien.

Cue Bun Boy. Never in my life would I eat at a sit-down restaurant by myself. This is not because I lack self-confidence or that I fear what people think, but I really like to multitask while I eat (talking, driving, or TV usually help me out with that). But when you're on a hot one, then you're on a hot one, and you need to sit the fuck down and eat. I flew in, seating myself on the patio so I could at least people watch. I didn't care what my waiter looked like; I just wanted them to feed me, goddammit.

Scrolling through emails, waiting for the damn server to come and give me a menu, I felt a new presence. (I'm so omniscient with caffeine. Honestly, I could solve world hunger on the stuff.) I darted my eyes away from my phone to look up and meet the perma-stoned[91] eyes of Bun Boy…my server. *Finally!* My initial thought was, *He better hurry up and bring me some food.*

As typical to my dining fashion, I gave him a couple of options for me to eat and told him to pick for me. (Servers probably hate this but I love it because then I don't really need to decide a damn thing.) Option

---

[91] Perma-stoned- adjective, *Slang*

1. Pertaining to the overuse of marijuana so much so that when the drug is no longer used, the user retains the permanent look of being intoxicated or "stoned."

one. Blank stare. Option two. Gapping gob. God, it took him forever to process what I had just asked him. *Why? Why? Why? I am hungry and I will kill you if you don't move your salty ass.* Finally, words began percolating from his throat to his tongue out of his lips. I probably stared. I definitely stared. A dagger stare. He took my order and slid away to the computer.

Five or ten minutes passed by and Bun Boy returned with my order. He had this look in his eyes, like he was scared of me or completely infatuated with me. I wasn't too sure what to make of it. All I remember thinking was, *This is going to be fun.* The struggle was real. BB had dropped my order down on the table and was still just standing there, like he was going to watch me eat my lunch...*Is he stoned? Am I supposed to eat and entertain him? What the hell am I supposed to talk to this cloud-puffer about?*

I took a bite as he lingered a few feet away, "So, how's that swell been?" I asked him, not knowing why he was still standing there.

"Ahh, dude.[92] It's been insane." He said rolling his body back like he was still on a surfboard.

I swallowed my first bite of tartine and continued, "Yeah, I was down at Big Corona and it was going off." I talked the talk.

BLANK STARE...Again. *Awkward...Maybe he's deaf?* I broke away from BB's bugged out eyes and clouded brain to take another bite. I was dying to scarf down my damn tartine, but I felt like I had to talk to this weirdo, "Have you gone out?" I said biting through the silence.

"Uh yeah, I like went out but just got wasted, like totally wasted, so then I just paddled past the break and laid back on my board and just like soaked it all in."[93]

"Wow, really?" I answered unimpressed.

"Yeah, the ocean is just like so powerful, and sometimes I just need to sit back and admire its beauty."

---

[92] I hate. HAAAAATTTTTTE. when guys say dude to a girl. I have a vagina. Say it with me...VAAA-GIIIN-Ahhh.

[93] I'm going to take the liberty of saying that he was stoned...very, very stoned.

Come on, you're stoned right? "Sounds like it's part of your soul," I egged him on.

"It is my soul," BB clarified with a philosophical glaze in his eyes.

Whoa, I think I'm like wasted now, too. "It's like a washing machine for you," I mumbled with a mouth full of tartine.

"Uh huh, yeah, it's like a washing machine for my soul."

God, that's not what I said, but sure, let's go with that.

To make a long, stoned story short, Bun Boy asked for my number and I gave it to him. *Why?* After forcing myself to waste away because of some non-existent "love" that never was and never would be, I thought Bun Boy was a perfect change of pace for me. Everything about him was slow—his speech, his observations, the way he blinked his eyes and took a breath. So, believe me when I say he was a nice change of pace.

Our first date was on Wednesday, December 17, 2014 (and on December 20, 2014, I almost died...dead serious[94]). True to modern wannabe hippie form, Bun Boy loved Thai and Indian food—which is to say, he was borderline obsessed with it. So it was pretty much a given that our first date revolved around one of the two, and BB decided on a Thai restaurant in a cool, new hip part of town. He had planned the entire date (which I would've never guessed he was capable of) and after dinner he drove us down to the harbor to walk through the thousands and thousands of Christmas lights that ornamented the otherwise dull boat docks.

For a week before our date, we had been texting nearly nonstop, and I hadn't been overly excited about BB. As arrogant as this sounds, I knew I had him from the moment we locked eyes and, to be honest, I wouldn't have been devastated had we never gone on a date. But there I was out with some guy that I usually wouldn't have glanced at twice, and I was enjoying myself. Bun Boy was so simple, so freaking simple. I looked at him under those twinkling Christmas lights and thought, *I never need to stress about this one.* So I accepted whatever (lack of) possibilities that were about to unfold with him, and decided to let him pursue me.

---

[94] No pun intended.

On December 20, 2014, only three days after I thought I had found the man that I could spend forever with (no, no, I never thought I could spend forever with BB, but for the thematics of this story—he was my soulmate) I almost died. This may sound like a random "Snapple Cap Fact," but I swear it ties in.

I was driving home from Long Beach with my mom to pick up my siblings so that the four of us could head over to our family Christmas party together. My mom and I had spent the day with my cousin's then six-month-old baby. We were headed down the 405 freeway about twenty minutes from home and had come to a complete stop; I was the last car in a line of traffic and then *BAM! BAM!* Some idiot hit my car, cascading me into the car in front of me. I was screaming bloody murder, and I felt bad for the ass that I was about to chew. (Ew, that came out wrong.) I was livid since three months earlier (two weeks before leaving for Colombia[95]) some dumb girl had sideswiped my car.[96]

I flicked my blinker right, and the three mangled cars pulled to the side. None of us had been hurt, but I was about to break someone. My mom got out of the car first to do damage control, as I flung my door open and hyperventilated in an attempt to control my urge to deck the stupid Ford Focus who caused the whole ordeal. The girl whose car I had struck got out, immediately screaming, "What the fuck?!"

"It wasn't my fault!" I bitched back.

"I know, it was that idiot's!" she said, pointing behind me.

Just then, a tall, twenty-something-year-old man emerged from the culprit's car. I was stunned. He was kind of cute, and for a second, I thought that maybe this would be like a "meet-cute" in a movie. You know, the oh-so-typical scene where the two main characters meet and immediately fall in love. *Maybe.* In my brain's attempt to realize this particular "meet-cute," I had forgotten about the now dully-colored Bun Boy and began to change my tone toward this obvious dumbfuck who had caused this accident.

---

[95] In hindsight I think this was a sign from the high heavens above telling me not to go...

[96] I think my car has bad juju.

He walked around his car, assessing the damage and snarled, "It's not my fucking fault." *Just kidding. You're a dick.* His arrogance and stupidity called me back to reality. There I stood in front of Dickhead's car with my mom and the other snarky betch standing to the side. Upon his obviously stupid remark, he slipped back into his car, started the engine and rip-roared his way from the scene of the crime.

As fate would have it, his breakaway wasn't clean. Without stopping, Dickhead swerved his car into southbound traffic, but instead of hitting the cars that stood in his way, he hit me. I had managed to push myself away from his revving engine, and just as I was flying through the air, I thought there must be a god (seeing as I wasn't hurt (yet)); but then, he finished me off by running over my right foot just as the left side of my body made sweet, passionate contact to the pavement. *Motherfucker.*

My body straddled the line separating the pull off area from raging freeway traffic. All I could think was, *thank god I bought life insurance from Daddy's Boy.*[97] *My mom will now be set for life and my siblings will have college completely paid for.* I was officially freaking out.

I could hear the rush of the traffic passing by; my mother's slow drawn out words, "It's okay honey, mommy's here" (no joke, she said that); the snarky betch screaming in Vietnamese on the phone to her mom (I wanted to shove her phone down her throat. She wasn't even hurt.); and my hatred for all of men rushed to my head at lightning fast speed. I didn't want to look at my body. I felt like I was bloody all over and I could feel my entire left side pulsate with pain and my right foot felt as though it was on fire. It was official: I hated men.

Two seconds ago, I had thought that Bun Boy was a prelude to this way hotter guy that had just mangled my car but now with a mangled body, BB wasn't looking so bad. While still on my back waiting for an ambulance, I pushed my mom far from traffic and snarled at every do-gooder that stopped to help (the irony being that, of course, all three people that stopped to help were men).

First, it was a father and son who had seen the whole thing happen and decided to start a conversation, during which the father continuously

[97] Oops, I forgot to mention that...I really am a sucker sometimes.

told me that I was going to go into shock. Finally, I had enough; he was distracting me from ruminating on my recently rediscovered hatred for men.

"I'm not going to go into shock. I have a tendency to pass out. It's called vasovagal syncope. Leave me alone, so I can focus on my breathing. I don't want to pass out!"

They didn't get the blatant hint until some off-duty CHP officer pulled over (since he saw me laying on the ground on the side of the 405) and asked them to step back. Initially, I thought, my savior.[98] Then he started to pester me, asking me all sorts of questions. He busted out his first aid kit and decided he would cut off my prized black Chuck Taylor's—they traveled through Medellin with me...they have sentimental value.

I cut my crying to tell him straight-faced, "No. You're not cutting off my Chucks." He didn't listen and proceeded to bring the glinting scissors closer to the fabric of my prized possession. "Don't!" I screamed.

"I need to cut them to examine your foot," he replied with a slight tinge of annoyance in his voice.

"Do NOT cut them off," I howled once again.

"I need to cut them," he said as he brought the harsh metal down onto the faded black fabric.

With pain singing through every ounce of my being, I ripped my foot from his hands and said, "Fine, I'll take them off myself."

My mom looked at me like I was such an embarrassment and the off-duty CHP officer looked at me like I was a nutcase as he continued to try and fight me to cut the damn shoe off. My foot was killing me, but it would be over my dead body on the side of the 405 that this copper cut my Chuck's. My mom gently said to him, "I think we should just take it off." Aghast, he agreed, and I got my way. *Bite me.*

Finally, the ambulance arrived. They locked me onto the gurney, locked that into place in the truck, clicked the doors shut and drove me to my hospital of choice (apparently, I wasn't about to die). I looked to

---

[98] No, not because he was hot. He was old. Ah shit, I should've thought of him for my single mom. Sorry mom.

the paramedic who was logging my information and thought he was cute, but after what happened just an hour before, I decided not to try my luck and stuck with Bun Boy. So I texted that simpleminded fool with a picture of my perfectly manicured (good thing I painted my toenails at my cousin's house earlier), yet mangled foot in the back of the ambulance and got all of the attention I wanted.

I figured that for the next few months of my life I would have to take it easy depending on the diagnosis the doc gave me. I was broken-bone-free[99] and I wasn't gushing blood, so they sent me home, and less than a week later, I hung out with BB.

BB wasn't my type. He was blond, not much taller than me and didn't have any aspirations. He lived in the garage of his parents' house and would continuously bitch and moan about "The Man," only he didn't pay attention to politics and was not up to date on current events (so what could he possibly have to say about The Man?). He had never gone to college and never wanted to go, which was fine, only he was completely content serving in not-so-high-paying restaurants. I guess I was still a bit lost in myself in that I settled with him for two whole months.

Even though he was immature and not my usual cup of tea, Bun Boy did have some redeemable qualities—superficial ones, at least. BB was a rather simpleminded old soul, lost in the hustle and bustle of an otherwise shallow modern world. Truly, he didn't care about money or material things, he just wanted the world in its physical and natural state and there was some sort of rare beauty in that to me. He had great taste in music. He enjoyed simple, yet fulfilling hobbies and he wasn't pretentious. BB would've been a better friend than "lover."

Against doctor's orders, Bun Boy and I went on endless hikes. We completely lost ourselves in nature, something I had never done before. Like two little kids, we would go off of the trails to climb rocks and pick flowers and leaves off of the plants to smell the smells of the lands we were exploring. It was amazing and completely novel to me. Here was

---

[99] Not true, a better specialist (shout out to you, you hunky doc) found a floating bone particle in my foot some months later.

this perma-stoned surfer kid, content and comfortable in who he was, and there I was, this "well-educated," "good girl"[100] restless in my lack of simple being. There was a deep beauty in all of his simplicity to me. I had never just been a raw version of myself. Before Bun Boy, I always had to wear at least mascara…I was afraid guys wouldn't be attracted to me if they saw me naked-faced. (How shallow is that?) No matter what I did or how I looked, he would always stare at me in this mesmerized way. Looking back, he was probably just stoned, but, regardless, it was intoxicating to feel "seen" in that way.

When we weren't hiking in the hills and mountains of our surrounding areas, we would be vegging out in the garage (a.k.a his bedroom). The winter was cold, and the insulation of the garage was poor. Besides the washer and dryer and the few paint cans that ornamented the walls of the garage, you couldn't tell that his bedroom was once the bedroom of sleeping cars. Various carpets and mandala tapestries enrobed the floor and "walls" of his makeshift bedroom. Two of his walls were composed of bookshelves that were chock full of books and stones and simple pleasures.

On the floor of his eclectically carpeted space was a record player with plastic crates full of both old and new records. When you laid back on his bed and peered into the rafters of the garage, your eyes were stopped by the string of blue-white twinkling lights he had wrapped across the beams from bookshelf to bookshelf. Some nights, when ice encrusted the air and warmth felt nearly impossible, Bun Boy would flick on the lights and spin on the record player. The warmth of the scratchy record player melted the frost and warmed our souls.

For a few weeks, I was in this blissful floating state. I wasn't in love with Bun Boy, and I knew we wouldn't and couldn't last forever, but the simplicity of life was too alluring to let him go. Of course BB, like the others, was far from perfect.

As our time together came to an inevitable close, BB became more distant. Honestly speaking, I didn't care. I had taken him for what he was and what he wasn't. He was someone who would teach you about

---

[100] Note that my "quotes" represent my convincing façade.

113

the joys of being a child again, curious in every sense of the word. He was someone who would get caught up in the descriptive words of a narrative and someone who would stay behind to pet a kitten when everyone else in the group kept walking toward more "adult" things. What he wasn't was a forever. He wasn't someone that I could spend my life with. He definitely wasn't someone who would start a successful business or who you could buy a house with. He wasn't someone for me, but that was okay because he was someone who showed me who I could be.

It was a couple of weeks before Valentine's Day, and I had never had a Valentine before so I was super excited. BB and I weren't texting/hanging out as frequently, but we were still "together." He had just returned from a weeklong impromptu camping trip to Big Sur, in which we hadn't spoken the entire time he was gone. His introduction text after not speaking for SEVEN days was, "I'm like so fuckin pissed."

I rolled my eyes and responded, "Why? What happened" My words were as empty as my concern.

"This stupid bitch lied to me," he stamped through text.

"What stupid bitch lied to you?"

"FUCK"

"?" I question-marked him, truly uninterested.

My stoner didn't respond through text. Instead, he called me to explain himself. (Oh, how adult of him.) Apparently some weeks before we had met he had slept with some girl (a.k.a. "Stupid Bitch"). Well, Stupid Bitch called BB in a panic on this particular night when he was "like flipping out" to tell him that she thought she had chlamydia even though her doctor told her it wasn't chlamydia. She was convinced (because she knew better than her doctor) that she had this wonderful STD and decided to share this lovely and enchanting bit of information with my braindead "boyfriend."

I would now like to say that before BB and I had sex for the first time I had asked him if he had recently been tested and that lying sack of sand said that he had and he was clean.[101] Obviously not. He kept

---

[101] Note: Men are liars.

going on and on and on over the phone, filling my ear with his pathetic sob story, not once asking me how I felt about this. *Um, yeah, hello. Do you realize that if you have chlamydia it means that I have motherfucking CHLAMYDIA?!*

I kept my cool and hung up the phone to save face before I ripped his off. Before leaving him with the empty scratching sound of an ended call, I told him that her doctor was probably right (like it's a really slim chance that this gynecologist was even right, but like, maybe? Right?) and that I was going to get tested the next day. Still flipping out, I left him on the other end of the call.

The following day, I calmly called my doctor's office. I attempted to explain to the receptionist that I immediately (as in "today" immediately) needed to make an appointment with my doctor, but she gave me the cold shoulder and tried to make an appointment for me a week out. *No, honey, that's not going to work.* So I was forced to freak out…not on her, just in general.

"No, I need the appointment for today," I reiterated.

"Sorry, that's not possible," she nasally replied.

"You don't understand, this is urgent," I said with more conviction.

"What is the purpose of your visit?" she entertained.

"I need a full STD checkup."

"We can schedule you for next week."

"NO. TODAY! My stupid boyfriend just gave me fuckin' chlamydia." I was all but shrieking now.

"Oh, okay. I can fit you in at twelve?" She was finally convinced that I needed a "today" appointment.

"Perfect. Thank you." *Click.*

Long story short, I didn't have chlamydia. In fact, I didn't have any STDs. *STUPID IDIOT.* I came back clean and so did my wonderfully, gullible Bun Boy.

We lasted up until the week before Valentine's Day, and then we mutually stopped talking to each other. There was no breakup, no fight, no love. We just weren't meant to be, and that was okay. Some time in the beginning of March he texted me, "I'm sorry for all of this." I wasn't sure what he meant since we hadn't talked in some many weeks, but

I accepted the good nature of his passing thought and let it slip away unanswered.

Oh, Bun Boy, why did I date you? I know why. He was thoughtless, not as in he didn't care about anything but as in I didn't have to think too hard to be with him. He was entrapped by the poetry of his foggy brain. I'd let him run his mouth and mind about some John Muir excerpt while I sat back and listened to his scratchy record player. We could hike mountains together without ever having to be near one another. We were a couple that leaned on each other for companionship but not in a romantic way. We would never kiss in public or hold hands or go away on vacations together. We were just there for each other so that the other person wasn't lonely.

Bun Boy wasn't my knight in shining armor, and I wasn't his queen. We certainly weren't soulmates. But for a little while, we were the right person at the right time for one another. Almost like we were moonlighting as soulmates. We were two kids figuring out life and love. And although it wasn't love, there was a sort of romance with him in that I rediscovered the simplicity of just being me, and I am grateful for that (even if he "gave" me chlamydia along the way).

A DANE & A DUTCH OVEN

"Save your acting for acting class."
You fucking bastard.

D uring my time dating Bun Boy, I had been offered a position at
an up-and-coming technology company, and after giving them
the go-around (mostly because I didn't want to be tied down to a desk
in some dingy office), I finally accepted their offer and began working
for them that February. (I figured BB and I weren't talking so I might
as well fill my time. Plus, I was about to be done with university, and I
knew I'd get bored.) True to my restless spirit's form, I barely lasted six
months in the office.

It wasn't because I couldn't handle the stress of the job or because
I hadn't a clue about the tech industry (there's this thing called Google
that taught me a lot). I didn't last simply because they had handed me
a stack of work that was supposed to last me through September and I
had it wrapped by May. Restless is an understatement—majority of my
last two months in the office were spent wasting away. I would watch
TED Talks eight hours a day all day and invent fictitious companies
for me to build out.

Of course I tried to take on another workload but my superiors
couldn't keep up with their own projects, let alone new things to give
me. Eventually, my wonderful Boss Lady decided that I should oversee
the Russian creative editor, since she always had grammatical errors…
Um, no thanks. I don't make this kind of money to babysit the Russian.

Finally, one day during a fit of boredom (and a lack of attention-grabbing TED Talks) I decided that I would follow my lifelong dream of acting. So I looked up the school I had previously been recommended by the producer I used to work for and made an entry audition for the following week.

Doomsday was upon me, and I told the Boss Lady that I had to leave early that day to run to L.A. to pick up my cap and gown from my university, which wasn't a complete lie considering I was going to walk in a few weeks. I had bought a new, sexy seventies-styled dress to audition as Rosalyn from *American Hustle*. I was soooo ready and so about to pass out.[102] But I headed out of the office, promising to myself that if I made it into the program I would leave that hellhole of boredom and pursue what I wanted.

I arrived at the studio, thudding my leopard-high-heeled-feet up the wooden steps. I was a wreck. No. Wreck is an understatement; I was a disaster. I signed my name on the dotted line and was called onto stage moments later. I began with what I thought was a convincing East Coast/New York accent but was expeditiously interrupted by a woman of charging presence. Then, I heard it—the truth in the lilt of her voice, the awful sounding vowels...she was from New York. *Damn it.*

"First of all, if you can't do a New York accent, then don't do a New York accent," she interrupted. "Start again," so I started again and was again interrupted. This time I was told to picture the words not as words but as images, so I tried and again was interrupted. Only now, I was asked how I felt about these words, these images, so I tried again.

"I like the honesty in your consideration," said my soon-to-be-favorite instructor. "I would love to have you in the program," and that was how I was invited into the program. *Did not expect that.*

Not to be one to break a promise (especially to myself), I quit my wonderfully short-lived career as a nine-to-fiver.

Prior to working for the tech company (if you can remember that far back), I worked at a snobby restaurant. Snobby or not, I had made

---

[102] I may have passed out giving a speech before and numerous times at the doctor's office.

some great networking connections there and decided I would hit one of said connections up to see if he needed a promising young assistant[103] who wanted to learn the real estate business as I waited for my acting career to take off. I figured I could take some real estate courses, get my license, kill it and not suffer like the rest of those poor, pathetic starving artistic souls.[104]

One afternoon, my boss and I went to lunch at the snobby restaurant where I was offered a serving job again. The manager pleaded with me, and I told him, I couldn't, that I needed to focus on the next stage of my life. Then the following night, my mother and I went to dinner at the snobby restaurant and the same manager asked me again, only this time in front of my mother who thought it to be a wise and noble idea: "Honey, you can make so much more money while you learn real estate." I thought about it and agreed, more money couldn't hurt.

THANK GOD! I took that serving job again, because it was no more than a month later that I got into a blowout texting fight with my short-lived real estate boss (and mentor). He told me that I needed to be at an open house alone (which is illegal if you don't have a license...I didn't have a license) and I told him that I couldn't because I had work at the restaurant. "You work for me," he said, really emphasizing the "me" in that statement.

I had already told him I couldn't work earlier that week. He was so obnoxious and had poor organizational skills so I told him, "I think it best if you find yourself a new assistant."

He didn't really like that statement and said some very aggressive things, but I didn't care. (He had bad breath anyway.) So, back to the snobby restaurant I went. I began picking up more shifts, working more hours and making more money than that shit ten dollars an hour the short-lived boss was paying me.

It was on a Friday night that I met Dane. I thought he was a drunk Irishman due to the way in which he enunciated his words—but, no.

---

[103] Note: I am an awful personal assistant because I hate being told what to do...in hindsight this was a stupid move.

[104] Hey guys! I don't really mean that. I love suffering with you.

Dane was Danish. The Danes have a drunken/deaf sounding slur when they speak English…no offense to the Danes.[105]

Before I go on, I would like to preface that Dane's real name was the Danish equivalent of my dead-beat father's name, Assdrew (minus the double "S" and adding an "N"). I should've taken the hint and stayed away.

Dane was at the bar with two others, a cute blonde woman and a witty Asian man. From the beginning, I thought that he was with the blonde girl and I knew that the other guy was married, so when Blondie asked me for my phone number because they wanted to go out with me when I got off of work, I wasn't perturbed by her request.

I got off early that night and responded to the text she had sent me. They were at the beach which was but a fifteen-minute drive, so I went home, changed and met up with them. When I arrived outside of the bar where Blondie had texted me to meet them at, she looked befuddled that I was there. Then Dane and a cue-ball-headed man came out of the bar. Dane greeted me much more enthusiastically than Blondie had, and Cue Ball was speaking in tongues (he was belligerent). The four of us walked to another bar just across the street, Cue Ball holding on to Blondie and Dane asking me a new question with each step.

We sat in the oversized leather chairs in front of the fireplace, and Dane stole away to grab us drinks. Cue Ball was all over Blondie, and I began to think that I had read her and Dane's relationship wrong. Then I started to think, *Oh shit. They're swingers. Why do I always get hit up by swingers?* When Dane sat himself down, he turned his chair to face me. Only me. Blondie looked livid but didn't say anything. *Okay, so they're not swingers.*

Dane and I talked and talked. Eventually, with growing concern for my life, I asked him how long he and Blondie had been dating. He laughed and corrected me by telling me that they all worked together and that she just thinks they have a special bond because she was born in Sweden and he is from Denmark.

---

[105] I mean you guys can at least speak two languages whereas most of us Americans can't even speak Mexican.

The night carried on, and they kept ordering drinks while I sipped on my one and only. (See, I learned from Poor Schmuck!) Soon it was time to go, I was going to drive myself home, and they were going to call for a taxi. I figured I would offer them a ride back to their cars (since their cars were halfway between where we were and my house), that way their Uber would be at least a little cheaper.

Coincidentally, Dane's hotel was down one of the cross streets to my house (about five minutes away), and Blondie and Cue Ball lived ten minutes apart from each other, but about twenty minutes from me. Dane asked me if I wouldn't mind dropping him off at his hotel and upon hearing this, Blondie freaked out and said she was going to give him a ride. This simple nothing turned in to a big something for this thirty-something-year-old woman. (She was too old to be acting like that.) We tried to justify the logic in our thinking to her. I didn't have hookup plans on the brain, but I certainly was not going to start a fight with this drunk woman to try and explain that.

We pulled into the parking garage where their cars had been left. Blondie stormed out of my car, slamming the door and starting the engine to her own car. Dane panicked and told her he would buy her an Uber because he didn't want her to drive. She wasn't having it and she really wasn't having it when drunken Cue Ball, stumbled out of my car and rolled into the passenger seat of hers.

It took everything in me to not laugh at this obviously immature, and now drunk, woman freaking out because she wasn't getting her way. Eventually, our blonde drama queen (for once, it's not me) caved and was forced to settle with Cue Ball. I began backing out my car, attempting to dodge the hate daggers shooting out of her. All I wanted to say to this sad woman was, "Look, I don't want him. He's cute but foreign isn't my style. It's too much drama." *Oh the irony.*

On that warm July night, the tires of my car crunched with pebbles as I pulled into the parking lot of Dane's hotel. He looked at me across the threshold separating us and asked me to come up for a glass of wine. It didn't come off as some random question or ploy to get me up to his room, I mean it was…but it didn't seem so. For the whole of the night, we had discussed our love for food and wine and the satisfaction you felt when you've perfectly paired the two. Earlier, Dane had excitedly told me about this bottle of wine he had just bought after searching for it for some time, and now he wanted to share it with me. I contemplated his face and the sincerity in his request. *Hmm, what shall I make of you?* So, I agreed and told him, "One drink." I parked my car, and we ascended the stairs to his chamber.

The almost vacuum-like seal of his door peeled open. Dane offered me a seat on the cranberry red couch that faced out to a window-framed parking lot while he poured our glasses of wine. He returned with a glass in each hand and sat next to me. We clinked our glasses and took a sip. Then he predictably leaned in to kiss me. I scooted back. I didn't want to kiss a man that didn't live here. (See, I learned that lesson from Colombiano. I'm learning!)

Dane had told me earlier that he was going to move to the U.S., but that wasn't enough for me. I thought about Colombia and the stupid mistakes I had made before and somehow reasoned to myself that a one-night stand was justifiable. So I leaned back over and kissed him. At first, the kisses were awful and laborious, but somehow, somewhere we found a rhythm. I let him take me to the bed twenty feet away and let him take me for my first one-night stand.

The dirty deed finished, and I gathered my things to leave. Dane was sincerely offended that I was leaving him. I told him that I couldn't be with someone who lived so far away. Again he told me that he was moving here. "Yeah but that's not enough," I said. I opened the door and walked out, presuming I would never hear from him again—and for once in my life, that didn't seem like such a big deal. I had just taken a man for what I perceived him as all he could be: a one-night roll in the hay and some good wine.

I got home some time in the wee hours of the morning and didn't think about him as my pillow cradled my heavy head and I drifted into a deep sleep. I hadn't held this man to some fantasy-like standards as I had with so many others before him, and I was completely content with my decision. Surprised, I awoke the next morning to a text message from Dane. He was asking me to spend the day with him. I politely declined and he continued to text me anyway. I refused to take him seriously; in fact, I figured all he wanted was sex, so I felt no desire or pressure to spend time with him. Only his text messages didn't mention his sexual desires in any way. I continued with my hardheaded ways and ignored the earnestness in his words.

Throughout the day he texted me, sending me pictures of him on the beach and telling me how much he loves California. Every once in awhile he would ask me to meet up with him again, suggesting I come join him at the beach and then for another drink, but I declined throughout the day and into the evening.

The following day was the same, only this was the day that I caved. Like the day before, he greeted me with a good morning text and again invited me out—to dinner this time. Initially I declined, but sometime around 12 p.m. I accepted and bought a new dress for a dinner date the following evening. *Oh, don't give me that look.*

Our date was set for Monday evening at a swanky restaurant I had only heard about. I drove myself to his hotel room and he drove us from there. Why did I accept the date? Was it because I wanted to buy a new outfit? Was it because I wanted attention? Was it because I knew that I was projecting past men onto him? I don't know. Maybe. Maybe it's one of those or a culmination of all of them. A more truthful truth would be that I was still extremely insecure in my experiences with men and knew it. I accepted the date because Dane seemed to be a stand-up gentleman. He was well-educated, hard working, and he knew how to be silly. He was eleven years my senior, but I felt like we saw eye to eye. Dinner was phenomenal both in conversation and cabernet. A bottle of Silver Oak and a robustly endless banter. Now, I liked him. A lot.

We finished our dinner, collected his car from the valet and drove back to his hotel. He was set to leave for Denmark in a few days and wouldn't return for another six to eight weeks, sometime in September. Unlike the last time, we made love. With bellies full of wine, a passionate dance unfolded. Sex with him wasn't like anything I had ever had before. To be even more clichéd, it was very European. Sex with him was raw, yet gentle. He was forceful, but thoughtful. Each and every move seemed calculated, but concupiscent. Dane was adventurous and made me feel like a goddess. He was the first man ever to make me come.

Although I can't say that that little bonus tingle was all his doing—I believe it to be all my own doing. For this was the first time that I didn't give a fuck. *Nope, no fucks given.* I went into our relationship as nothing more than a fun time. Even if Dane was grand and all that mambo jazz, I cared about myself more. For once, I was my focus in a relationship and I didn't care if I disappointed him, turned him gay, or gave him blue balls. I wanted what was best for ME. It wasn't because of his impeccable pecker skills or his sweet, dirty words whispering in my ears. It was me, my self-confidence and finally discovering the ease of awakening my sexuality. (God, this is the absolute cheesy truth.) I had somehow become a woman.

We remained entangled in his bed for some hours after. I didn't want to let myself slip too far into the blissfulness of it all, but it was so difficult because I already knew I had fallen for him. *Dammit, Dax.* I unraveled our woven bodies and told him it was time for me to drive home. Without question, he dressed and wished that I would spend the night with him, but once again I ignored his truthful words and listened to the lies of the insecurities that rang through my head. He walked me to my car in the dead of night, kissed me goodbye and wished me a safe drive. I arrived back at my house with a text message from him, inviting me to lunch two days later because he wanted to see me one last time before he left. I smiled to myself in my darkened house at the thought of his words.

As planned, we met two days later at the place where we had first encountered one another—my snobby restaurant. We sat at the bar and ordered lunch. It was bittersweet. Dane was so attentive, and I was so distant. I couldn't stop thinking about how this would be the last day that I ever saw him. I began regretting our intimacies and letting my guard down. He sensed my scattered thoughts and reached across the table, "I want to keep talking to you." I half-smiled, unsure of how I should respond. "I need to see you when I come back," he said to ease my worries further. I turned my head down and then the bill came. Lunch was over, and it was time for him to leave.

We walked out together, Dane confident and content and me unsure and insecure. Suddenly my insecurity found my words, "We need to talk every day. Otherwise, it won't be real."

He grinned ear to ear, "Of course we will speak every day."

Valet brought his car around, he kissed me and drove away. *This is the end*, I thought.

A man of his word, Dane and I spoke every day. Even with the nine-hour time difference, we managed to make it work, speaking around my bedtime as he took the train to work, and then again when I awoke and he was heading out of the office. There was a rhythm and mutual respect. Dane gave me all of the attention I could desire from a long distance, and I did the same with him. But talking wasn't enough, and soon I began talking to another guy, a boy whom I should've never been with but who gave me the physical attention that I craved so much from Dane.

When Dane returned, I told him the truth. I told him what it was that I actually wanted. I wanted a serious relationship, one that would allow the both of us to grow and could lead to more. I was done with the silly games and lies of those that had come before him. He was upset that I had hooked up with an ex and told me that he wanted me all for himself. I cried. No one had ever said that they wanted me and only me.

We became inseparable. Only Dane's inevitable return back to Denmark could break us away from each other. Every night was spent with one another, and we would have lunch together on days that he didn't have business lunches or meetings. He set his own schedule since he was the CFO for some big company and had a lot of pull around the office. So, we had a lot of time to spend together. Our nights were spent at swanky restaurants, stuffing ourselves with overpriced food and overindulging in what seemed to be an endless bounty of alcohol. We were having the time of our lives; everything just seemed so perfect. I had stopped talking to the boy I should've never talked to in the first place, and I put all of my eggs in Dane's basket. Even with the great distance of thousands of miles, our relationship was easy. Everything between us seemed like it was meant to be.

Sometime in October, or maybe November, when Dane returned to me for the third time, we were all set to enjoy a three-day weekend together. For dinner, he had decided on an upscale Indian restaurant overlooking the Pacific Ocean. We stuffed our faces full. Our bellies looked like those of malnourished African children—I know, that's a horrible comparison—bloated with naan and cocktails and chicken and Indian spices and god knows what else. We nearly rolled ourselves out of the restaurant and down the toll road back to his hotel.

When we got back to his room, we both laid ourselves out across the bed in an attempt to find a comfortable position in which our food could digest. I was dying—WE were dying. Every position made the copious amount of food in my body feel like the foot of a baby elephant crushing down on me. Dane rolled over to kiss me, our bloated bellies bumping into each other. We laughed as he tried once again to successfully kiss me. Somewhere in our drunken state, we decided that sex would help our food digest (WRONG, it was so awful!) and soon after, we fell asleep.

The next morning I awoke myself with a fart. Yup, you heard me correctly. I farted myself awake. To make matters even worse, we had fallen asleep with our naked bodies wrapped up tightly, Dane spooning me from me behind with one of his legs between my legs. What does that mean? It means I farted on his leg. I laid there with my ass still facing him in a silent panic. What the hell was I supposed to do? Claim the cursed vibration? Admit that this unfiltered morning trumpet came from me? I felt him wiggle his leg out from between mine. *God, he knows I just farted on him!* I stiffened up. *Stupid Indian food.* I pretended to be asleep and stayed "asleep" until he left the bed and got out of the shower and "woke" me up. I was so embarrassed.

We parted ways that morning but would reunite later that night since we had plans for dinner again. *Oh, my poor stomach!* Dane told me he had some work to do and that I would be too distracting if I stayed at the hotel with him. I wasn't offended by it—that's how it always was when we were together, so I left and went home. I didn't mind. I obviously needed time to let loose after my little morning trumpet performance. Not to mention, I also needed to confide in my mother that I had just ripped ass on some man's leg. I figured my mom would know how to handle such an awkward situation—but alas, I was wrong. Instead, she just laughed hysterically to the point that she wasn't able to breathe. *Thanks mom, I'll remember that.*

Later that night, night number two of our three-day weekend, we went out to Mastro's Ocean Club. Dane wanted to find new restaurants to take potential clients to, so he named me his official guinea pig. I didn't mind being his rodent if it consisted of us going to some bomb ass (obviously I was the bomb ass) restaurants. Plus, I loved getting dressed up!

Our reservations weren't until 9:00 p.m. since Mastro's was completely booked, and Dane was a little irritated that we had to wait so long. I convinced him to go an hour and a half earlier than our reservation in hopes that we might be able to get in sooner. We couldn't so we headed to the bar, and I got drunk before dinner. *Oopsie doopsie.* Finally, we sat down at our table next to some snotty Botoxed bitch who kept checking out Dane's watch. (That's what we like to call a gold digger in Orange County.) The service was horrible, but luckily for us, the waitress was at least mediocre enough to get in our wine order. I didn't care about dinner anymore even though we eventually ordered and stuffed ourselves silly for the second night in a row.

Like the night before, after eating like heifers and eating some cows, we headed home feeling rotund enough to roll ourselves there. And like the night before, we made sweet, passionate, glutinous love with all of the meats and macaroni cheesing through our insides.

Shake, shake, shake—Dane's keys jiggled in the lock of his room. One more hard jig and the door swung open. We poured into the funneling darkness of the room. He pushed me against the wall. My stomach mooed and I moaned as he spilled some alcohol-induced idioms into my ears—salting me, squeezing me, drinking me, intoxicating me. I was buzzing. Our liquid bodies cascaded against the scratchy cold surface of the hotel walls. I demanded to be taken to the bed (simply because I couldn't bear the calf-sized weight in my gut), where I ordered a cannoli...*Holy cannoli, give me wiener or give me death—I mean give me wine, or give me death.* He whipped out that cream-stuffed pastry and I shook with sweet, sweet anticipation. He poured some robust words into my thirsting ears and satiated my sugar-withdrawals. He had stuffed me and then I hit the sack.

Unfortunately for me (and maybe him), I farted myself awake for the second morning in a row. Only this time (luckily) we weren't cuddling, but I was laying on my side with my ass fired and ready facing him. *Lovely.* Again, like the morning only the day before, I laid there dead still. Thankfully, the sweet Danish man pretended to be asleep—at least, I hoped that he was still asleep. And once again, in what is apparently my modus operandi of wake-up farts, I pretended to be asleep until he got up to shower and "woke" me up. I was dying and cursed at my gluttonous belly. Like the day before, I left him so he could continue his work and I could go home and get ready for our already planned evening (and release my ass cannon).

It was like clockwork, I arrived back at his hotel some time around 5:00 p.m. to have dinner and drinks at the beach. This time, I picked the restaurant. I prepared myself to say no to all of his indulgent food requests. I would eat salmon and have one or two glasses of wine with room to share dessert. Only one dessert, not two, not three—one! Doggone it; I was going to do it! And oh boy did I do it. I successfully said no to all of the extra food (mostly because I didn't want to fart myself awake again).

Dinner was wonderful, and, best of all, my breathing wasn't slow and labored. I could stand and sit without feeling like I was going to pop the seams of my dress. And I had room for dessert. *Oh Butter Cake, how I love you.* We left the restaurant happily full and headed back to the hotel. That night we made sweet, sweet love without our tummies mooing and slopping about with steak and liquor.

"Brrrrrrrrttttttt," I awoke. *Ah shit, did I do it again? God damn it, Dax...No wait, that wasn't me!* I looked over to my Danish lad and realized with his legs cranked up into the air, he had ripped a big one. *Don't make any sudden movements.* Once again, I laid still but this time it was for his sake, not mine. It took everything in me to not laugh. I wanted to laugh so badly, just thinking how embarrassed I had been the past two mornings before and now, here we were, almost even in our fart tally. *You can't let him know that you're awake.*

From the corner of my half-opened eye, I saw him freeze, then he slowly began to draw his legs down onto the bed. His body moved like that of a lion on the prowl for its prey, cautiously moving through the tall grass leaving its victim (that would be me) undisturbed. I played opossum, hoping that he would pass by me. It worked! He slithered his legs flat with the surface of the mattress and rolled over. He never knew that I was awake to hear him in his gaseous state. *Woo!* True to the routine of our mornings together, Dane got out of bed, showered and kissed me good morning, only now our relationship was at that next level: we were so much farter (I mean, further) into it with one another.

Neither one of us ever mentioned the infamous three-day farting spree. We carried on our relationship as normal—a couple of weeks together and even more weeks apart. I started getting used to the rhythm of it and I finally began to trust the distance. Before Dane, I thought every man was a cheater, a liar or a dead-beat. He did the work to build my trust, and believe me, it took work for me to trust someone. I felt like I was literally handing him my heart and asking him to not crush it. I was in it and trusting it, trusting him, trusting where it might lead.

Well, somewhere along the line in our happy journey together, we started this joke. This sick, disgusting joke in which he would mention Denmark, and I would ask him about his wife and kids. I know, I know—it's so awful—but it seemed funny at the time because there was absolutely no evidence of him having a family.

Until one day, a few days before he was slated to return to his home country, I told him I wanted to spend a week with him in Denmark. Everything in the room changed, Dane's body got stiff and his brow furrowed in a panic. "No."

I laughed, thinking he was joking. "Come on, you know you want me to come see you and your family," I jested back.

But then I saw the alarm on his face as he searched for an excuse. "You can't come…"

"Why?" I could feel the tension of an ugly truth clouding my brain.

"Because it's not the right time," he spat back.

"Well, why not?" I was curious now that he was so adamantly refusing.

"It's really cold this time of year," he lied.

"I don't care. I'll buy cute winter clothes."

"I'm really busy with work," he tried again.

I had heard that lie before, and I knew all too well what it meant so I let the moment pass, hoping that my brain was just overreacting in an attempt to protect my heart. I could feel myself shut down, but I didn't want Dane to see my brain think these thoughts. Within seconds, I began to dissect every moment we had together and every moment that we had apart.

To this day, I am not sure which was true: what Dane was telling or what felt way more real in my head. What I can tell you is that the truth I had in my head eventually became our reality. I'll explain:

Unknowingly to Dane, that conversation had filled me to the brim with insecurity.

Is there someone else? Does he have a family? Am I the other woman? Is that why he needs me to leave the hotel room so he can "work"? Is he calling his family then? How could I have done this to someone? How did I not see this before?

Every moment between us now screamed of dishonesty. I began thinking about every time we had contact with each other when we were apart, how routine it was—businesslike, transactional. When I had called him to FaceTime, he would refuse the call if he was at home and then call me back always from the rooftop of his building, and, for the most part, the only time we spoke on the phone was when he was on his way to work or returning home from work.

I began to think about his lack of social media and how often he traveled for his job. Denmark to the United States and then back to Denmark then to Singapore and then back to Denmark to start the cycle over again. I began to carve through the scuba diving trip he had taken to Gile Air with his "friend" that never had a name or a gender and how during that air-sucking underwater adventure, we never spoke (which was uncharacteristic for us). My head was a mess with clues and evidence that I had never put together before. *Am I overreacting? Was I so blind to all of this? How could I be so stupid?*

I didn't know what to do with the knowledge I had uncovered, all the doubt that came with it like a shitty freebie. I struggled with accepting and refuting the facts. Lost, I hadn't a clue of what to do with myself. As always, I shut off. I decided that it would be best if I stopped talking to him and only responded to him if and when he contacted me. *It's not like I have to worry about running into him. He's gone. This'll be easy.* He didn't seem to notice which made my frustrations grow infinitely more. His lack of attention assured me all the more that there was someone else. I died thinking about me being the other woman who was destroying a family. A family that I still wasn't sure existed.

Time passed, and my thoughts settled. It was now December, and Dane had returned to California. I was mixed with emotions at the thought of seeing him after making so many realizations. In fact, I had concluded that I needed to end things and began speaking to another man (who would later lead me down the same rabbit hole of lies). I declined Dane's attempts to meet up with me, but soon he broke through my hard candy shell. He asked me what was wrong and I finally let all of my fear spill out of me.

I answered him with a question, the thing I wanted to know most: "Do you have a wife and kids?"

He pulled my distant body into his chest, "No, I told you that was a horrible joke."

"Then why couldn't I see you in Denmark?" I asked again.

"I'm busy, I told you," he said it in a way that was too abrupt to make me feel any better.

"Why didn't we speak when you were in Gile Air?"

"I was on vacation." *So does that mean you were on vacation from me?*

"Are you going to move to the U.S.?" I asked in hopes of uncovering his lie.

"I'm trying," he answered coyly.

I sat in silence, contemplating each screaming emotion thudding its way in to my consciousness.

"I think I'm falling in love with you," he said grabbing my head and whispering it hot into my right ear.

"No you're not," I responded dryly, as though there was no way he could refute my negation.

We didn't say anything more. I wasn't convinced by his "love" but I stayed the night with him anyway.

We made dinner in his new apartment, purchased on the company's dime so Dane could stay somewhere more homey during his time in California, and went to bed. I didn't want to have sex with him; I couldn't bear the thought of his cheating dick. It wasn't love anymore—but the funny thing is that I never thought that what we had was love, even when he whispered it into my ear. I never responded. I could never love a lying man. I walked into his bedroom with anger in my heart. Wanting so badly to give him the benefit of the doubt. Wishing I could find the truth.

But the truth found me first.

As we got ready for bed, Dane went into the bathroom, shutting the door as I remained on the outside, undressing myself. He had left his phone on the desk across the room, so I went to move it to his bedside table since I knew his alarm for the morning was on his phone. I'd like to clarify before I go any further, I would never intentionally go through someone's phone—it's not my style and even if I wanted to, I couldn't. I think it is invasive, but when I grabbed Dane's phone, his screen lit up with a flurry of messages from Anna. *Who's Anna?* All of the words were Danish but he had taught me enough to know certain words. *Elsker, knus* and *kys* highlighted in my brain. Love, hug and kiss.

There was my answer, my answer to what I had felt to be true laying in the palm of my hand. The man that I had questioned myself for trusting was just behind a door ten feet away and at any moment that door would swing open bringing his lying mouth back to me. *Stupid idiot, you should learn to make your messages notify you with only the person's* name.

I grabbed my phone, debated taking a picture of his screen and clicked a photo of this Anna's message. I would translate it later and would decide afterwards if I was right. I knew his sister's name but didn't remember his mother's. The bathroom door creaked open just as the back of his phone slid across the surface of his nightstand. I backflipped myself over the bed,[106] squeaked past him and walked into the bathroom. *Hopefully that distracted and/or confused him enough.*

The door to the bathroom clacked shut, but my mind was ajar with thoughts. *Do I leave now? What if it's nothing? What if Anna is his mom? What's his mom's name? I know his sister's name, but what is his mom's name?* I flushed the toilet with my speculations still swirling and walked out.

Dane set his phone down to look up at me. "What's your mom's name again?" I asked him. Immediately, he knew that I now knew and evaded my question. I am…not sly. I pretended to be oblivious to it all as we turned off the lights and said goodnight. There was no way in hell that I would be able to fall asleep now.

I laid there in that coffin of a bed with my eyes flickering back and forth as each and every harassing thought propelled me further and further away from sleep. I kept thinking back to this long text message that I had discovered not by choice but by pure coincidence… or perhaps it was fate? Finally, my nagging curiosities got the best of me and sometime in the early hours of the morning with Dane serenading us with his snores, I translated the entire message. I was right. I had been right the entire time.

The message wasn't short, but it was simple enough to understand that Anna wasn't some passing fling. She had written Dane to thank him—to thank him for the wonderful note that he had hidden away somewhere in her makeup bag. I found myself getting caught up in the romance of their affair. Hiding a love note in a woman's private toiletry bag, it was so unexpected. And I could only imagine her blissful giddiness upon the note's discovery. She told him how she missed sitting on the docks watching the sunset with him, how she missed getting their morning cups of coffee together, and how she

---

[106] Think more "Ace Ventura" than "Olympic Gymnast."

couldn't wait until she saw him again. The hazy shades of red, orange and pink sunsets started to color my eyes and then the purple calm of the cold rising morning sun mixed with the scent of warm coffee filled my sappy soul. She had kissed him and hugged him and she most definitely loved him.

As I lay there silently panicking about how I would react, I fell asleep. The next morning Dane turned to kiss me, but I couldn't bring myself to do the same. "You're being a brat," he said and walked out of the room. *Hmm yeah, I'm a brat...I guess being a cheater is better.* I ignored his childishness and packed my things to leave. I'd figure out how to deal with him later. I wasn't exactly sure of how to handle this situation—I mean, *yes*, I violated his privacy, but he broke my trust! Plus, I truly thought that he would text me for the awful way our morning had transpired.

He didn't. So, I caved and texted him. I didn't text him because I longed to be with him or because I thought that he was the one, or that we could work things out, or he would leave Anna for me. Surprisingly, I didn't think any of those pathetic thoughts. It was simple: I texted him because I wanted an answer. Simple enough, right? But he didn't respond.[107]

It took him hours, nearly a whole day. Hours upon hours of waiting and deciding that I wasn't in the wrong. I had been right all along, but it was bittersweet confidence that came over me. Bitter because I was right, bitter because it was done, but sweet because I knew the truth and sweet because I had the power to walk away from it all. Still, the bitterness of knowing the truth outweighed the sweetness of the relief of knowing the truth.

I held my breath when my phone finally rang. "Hello?" I answered.

"Hey, I was in a meeting," Dane replied.

"Oh." I didn't know what else to say.

"I know you went through my phone," he said with great accusation.

---

[107] Note: A guilty man will always give you a guilty answer and silence is the ultimate guilty response.

"I didn't go through your phone, I only saw the messages on your locked screen," I corrected.

"You were going through my phone all night." *You wish, you arrogant prick.*

"No I didn't." I began to cry. I was so disappointed in myself. *Why did I text him? I should've just left everything alone and disappeared from him.*

"Save your acting for acting class."

Whelp, that set me off, "I'm not acting you stupid fuck, I'm upset."

"Stop crying."

"I can't believe you would lie to me," I said as I raised my voice to mask my tears.

"I never lied."

My ass you never lied. "Who's Anna?" I angrily whispered into my phone.

"She's my friend."[108]

"Why have I never heard of her? That message was not a message from a friend!"

"You translated it?" He acted like he was actually surprised.

"What was I supposed to do? I couldn't sleep."

"You're so dramatic."

"And you're a liar." I was starting to hyperventilate.

All I could think about was decking this dumb sack of shit square in his nut sack.

"You really are a drama queen." *I hope you get fucked by a drag queen.*

"I can't talk to you anymore." I said it plain and straight.

"Whatever. You know you're overreacting." (Yes, he thought he was so cool and Californian because he said "whatever.")

"I don't think I am," I said in-between the deep breaths I was taking to avoid passing out.

The call ended, as did our relationship, when I blocked and deleted Dane from my phone. In hindsight, it was for the best—and he should thank god every day that this ended over the phone because I was about

---

[108] Can someone please teach men to be more original with their lying?

to Lorena Bobbitt his ass. Besides, he was going to make me fat with all of the overeating we indulged in. And who knows what else he would make me if that twisted, dishonest relationship continued. (Crazy. The word you're looking for is crazy.) Of course I was still hurt by him, but unlike so many before, I didn't dwell on what I thought I had "lost." I moved on from Dane to bigger and better (and by better, I mean worse).

THE $*@^

And you wonder why I hate my real name?

Some of you are about to read this and think I fucked my boss. I would like to clarify right now: I didn't fuck my boss. I began what I thought was an honest relationship with a man who used to be my boss, months after I had left the company and months after having no contact with anyone from the company, including him.

Ah, I know what you're thinking, I left the company because I wanted to be with him. Not the case. I left the company because I was twenty-two, fresh out of college and I felt impassioned to pursue a creative path. Honest! I left a well-paying position at a very successful startup company to pursue acting. *Ew, why?* Call me crazy but who wants to be chained to a desk when you aren't running the show? I would also like to clarify now that I never intended on dating him, we never had a forbidden office romance, and I didn't want him for his money (and I sure as hell never wanted to be mixed in with the actual bimbos that he dated).

Some of you may hear all of this and still think that I'm lying and that's fine. In all of my trials and tribulations I have encountered in my search for love, one man stands out as my greatest mistake—actually, my greatest embarrassment.

Freud and Jung said it, and I did it. I, Dax Marie, began to see a man who was almost identical to a man whom I never want to associate myself with: my father. And just like my dad cheated on my mom, this boss man was also a cheater. So, I guess his alias shall be El Tramposo—that means the cheater in Spanish. *Ooo original.*

During my time at the company, I watched him tear his family apart through an interoffice relationship with a girl who worked in our out of state office. My dad cheated on my mom with his secretary. El Tramposo drank a lot, my father drinks a lot (last I checked, he had pancreatitis). They both have/had successful companies.[109] The only difference between the two? El Tramposo liked downers and Daddy Dearest likes uppers. *We should have a Socratic seminar based on weed versus speed.*

Why then? Why did I allow myself to be pursued by a man whom I thought was a disgusting piece of shit, to begin with? Why? I knew from the beginning that he was a cheater. Unfortunately, I had known most of his dirty little secrets since my best friend during the time I worked at the company was his personal assistant. *Personal indeed.* I asked myself over and over again once I came to discover a truth that I had already known. Why did I do it? Why did I allow it to happen? He was intellectually brilliant and socially retarded. So why? Why would I want to involve myself with someone who has developmental issues?

The truth is, I know why. I thought that he was a changed man, a sinner turned saint. We met one night, five months after I had left the company. After he had begged for me to grab a drink with him, after confiding in me that he had cut himself off from everyone he used to know, and after I had handed him his ass over a string of purposefully worded text messages.[110] After all of that, he still wanted to grab a drink with me. So, I met him for a beer. *Mistake.*

I walked into the Yard House and scanned the bar. No El Tramposo. Then, the November air whooshed in through the door behind me. I

---

[109] El Tramposo may have lost his by now, too, since he was under council by the other partners for the bounty of sexual harassment charges he had against him. I know of at least three.

[110] Yes, I told him I thought he was a pig in these texts and that everything he had done was wrong. I told him that his kids would grow up to despise the man that ruined their picturesque upbringing. Ironically, I told him everything that I had told my father years ago.

turned around and saw what appeared to be a changed man. He looked humbled, like he finally understood what it was like to lose. He seemed as though he sincerely regretted his crimes against the innocent lives that he had toyed with so carelessly. His eyes met mine, and before I knew it, his arms were wrapped around my body in a wholesome embrace.

We sat at one of the bar tables where he spilled his guts to me. How he had broken up with his mistress, how he was being sued for sexual harassment, how his ex-wife was moving back to their home state with the children, how one of his business partners disappeared after not being able to handle the temptations that came with all the money they were making, and how he wanted nothing to do with women or dating.[111] I sat and listened, occasionally commenting, and openly embracing the trap.

I never wanted to be romantically involved with El Tramposo, but I thought no harm could be done with friendship—only I was incapable of limiting myself to a friendship. I fell hard, and that was my fault. I allowed myself to be mixed in with all of his lies and bimbos. I knowingly blinded myself to the truth. *That was dumb.* I could sit here and argue that it was his fault, that he's the world's greatest liar, or that it was my romantic soul's fault and that all I wanted was to be loved, but none of that is completely true. Here's the truth accurately told through cliches: *people never change* and *it takes two to tango.* What does that mean? It means that El Tramposo never changed. He could never change. His shit was so far ingrained into his being that five months' time could never make a man like him wake up. All I wanted was for ET to be a changed person, a better human being, so I created a better version of him in my head and projected it onto the real him (sounds like I was trying to save my dad). *It takes two to tango.*

So what was the big climactic downfall? Bet you're titillating with anticipation…Whelp, here it is: Some weeks after hanging out with El Tramposo, my gold-digging ex-best-friend (who shall henceforth be known as Gold Digger) and his personal assistant texted me after

---

[111] Not all of this was true. In fact, El Tramposo manipulated the details quite a bit.

literally months of not talking. Out of the blue,[112] she invited me to the company's Christmas party and said that she had asked El Tramposo if I could go. He had agreed, so I agreed. I brought it up to him later that night when we had gone out to sushi, and he said, "Of course I want you there." I told him that I wanted to keep us on the down low since I wasn't ready to publicize it yet in front of all of my former colleagues. He agreed once again. So it was settled, and there was nothing to worry about…or so I thought.

Two days before the Christmas party, El Tramposo nonchalantly told me as we were watching a movie at his house, "Babe,[113] I forgot to tell you. I forgot that I had promised some girl from our Texas sales office that she could come to the party, so she's going to be my date."

Uh, okay.

"I'm sorry, babe." He hugged me.

You cheeky bastard. "For what?" I asked with the façade of calm.

"I completely forgot," he acted.

"Please, it's better this way. Now no one will suspect anything." I reassured myself more than him.

"Ah, babe I feel bad but I couldn't say no to her. They're some of our best sellers."

My ass. "It's fine, I'm not mad at all," I lied.

Fast-forward to that Saturday. Gold Digger had called me to get ready at her house with her boyfriend and the office gays.[114] I came dressed and ready because I hate getting ready with people. I could tell she was prying hard. She kept hinting that El Tramposo was bringing some "wonderful" girl (named my real name) from Texas to the party and that he always talked about how "in love with her" he was. He would refer to her around the office as his Unicorn. *Gag.* I kept my

---

[112] Note: This was not out of the blue, Gold Digger had a nasty habit of tracking the numbers that El Tramposo was texting since she had access to his cellphone plan. Ridiculous.

[113] Please fucking note: I hate "BABE."

[114] Please note the irony in this grouping, we later found out that Gold Digger's boyfriend did gay porn. Poor guy, she was a bitch to him and probably forced him into doing it and then acted like she never knew.

cool and didn't respond. I acted genuinely happy for him. If this was his dream girl, then so be it. I would sincerely be happy for him. So my happy train kept chugging away and was about to arrive at cruel reality. They finished getting ready and we left for the party.

We had to get to the venue a little early since Gold Digger was tasked with making sure everything was in order (comes with the personal assistant territory). Everything was set and ready, which meant we could start drinking. Then, about fifteen minutes before the party started, El Tramposo called Gold Digger and told her to go buy tampons for his Unicorn since she had unexpectedly started her period. *What kind of mother doesn't teach her daughter to always have backup? Stupid.* Lovely. That meant I had to go with Gold Digger to buy tampons for El Tramposo's Unicorn.

This was a new low; I was going to buy something for her to plug her "unexpectedly" bloody vagina. *Bite me.* To top it off, we were already buzzed on top of a hill which meant we had to waltz our high-heeled, tight-dress-wearing asses all the way down the hill to get the majestic Unicorn's tampons. We hiked down our mountain and Gold Digger asked El Tramposo to pick us up but he refused when we got to the bottom and found no tampons. *Asshole.* So my stupid ass had to volunteer to share a tampon with the Unicorn because, of course, I was also on my period. *Oh the irony of our synchronized cycles.*

I took a tampon from my eighteen dollar Target clutch and watched as she majestically slid *my* tampon into her stupid Alexander McQueen clutch. I knew what that meant, and Gold Digger knew I knew what that meant.[115] I knew El Tramposo's cheating ways were still flowing strong through his poorly maneuvered dick. Gold Digger stood there knowing everything. *Oh, well.*

At that moment, I vowed to myself that I would stay away from El Tramposo. I wanted nothing to do with him and, honestly, I was okay with just letting him and his Unicorn float away. I felt perfectly

---

[115] El Tramposo is a dumbass and kept asking me what I wanted for Christmas which I would reply with "nothing," to which he would reply, "how about an Alexander McQueen bag?" I never got a gift.

capable of not saying a thing to him or anyone else. I mean, it's not like I was going to be teeming with sweltering rage later that night, right? RIGHT??

An hour or two into the party and perhaps a few drinks too many, El Tramposo came up to me and whispered, "You look gorgeous." I smirked and walked away. I still had face to save. No one knew except for maybe Gold Digger and our token gays (or at least that's what I like to believe). The party continued, unhitched. It was glorious…then came the afterparty.

Welcome to the "cool kids" party, only a select few of us were invited to the afterparty which wasn't saying a lot considering they decided to continue the party at one of the most infamously disgusting dive bars in Orange County. At that point, I had sobered up, so I decided to drive. Gold Digger and her boyfriend rode in my car. Neither one of them could keep their eyes open even though it was her damn idea to continue the party. She had a raging, chronic case of what the kids like to refer to as FOMO.[116]

In we walked, the drunks and I. Just as we passed through the front door, El Tramposo was macking on Unicorn. *Keep your cool.* He broke away from the kiss to sloppily make eye contact with me. I beelined to the bathroom behind Gold Digger. I wanted nothing to do with the potentially dramatic scene El Tramposo could've caused and since Gold Digger was most definitely going to vomit.

Gold Digger booked it into the one-person bathroom as I politely declined her offer to go in with her. We had been out drinking before, and I knew all too well that if I went in that bathroom with her, I may be subject to puke speckles on me.

As I stood outside the bathroom door, listening to make sure she didn't pass out on the toilet (she had done it before and I had to crawl under the wet, toilet paper infested floor to pull up her pants and hold back her hair as she vomited), El Tramposo snuck up behind me. Reaching in to hug me, "Hey," the creep said.

Avoiding his hug, I replied with a curt, "Don't touch me."

---

[116] Fear of missing out. It's an insult.

His face got very coy and as his eyes glassed over with a subdued rage. He honed in on me, "What the hell. She means nothing to me." He tried to whisper it into my ear.

"You're disgusting. Don't fucking talk to me." Oops! Did I say that out loud?

"You're crazy." He shouted in my face.

Oh? I'm crazy? Pissed, he stormed away just in time for Gold Digger to open the door for me to go to the restroom. *Woo, she just missed it.* I hovered over that yellow-stained pot a little shaken up. Who the fuck did he think he was? Dirty bastard thought he could play me like that?! *FUUUUCK YOU.*

Gold Digger and I walked back to our table to find her boyfriend, the gay porn star, passed out in the corner and the bouncers kicking him out. We didn't want to leave. The music was just starting to liven things up and we were about to tear up that dance floor. We didn't know what to do with his drunk ass...*Ah, I've got it!* I walked Gay Porn Star out to my car which was parked right in front of the bar and tucked him in with some blankets, "Don't leave. I am going to lock my car so the alarm will go off if you try to open the door."

Poor guy, he was so drunk he barely knew which way was up, "Uh, okay. I'll stay."

I made sure to cover his face with blankets, too, just in case the cops walked by and were wondering why some drunk adult film star was sleeping in a car. *He's taken care of.*

I ran back into the bar, and we danced the night away. Seriously. I didn't think about El Tramposo and he sure as hell didn't try to bother me after I told him off. Gold Digger and I just had fun. The bar closed and I drove everyone home, thinking that I would never have to see any of them ever again. Well, at least that's what I hoped.

Ring, ring, ring.

Surprise!!! Cue my oh-so unwelcome, unscheduled wakeup call at 8:00 a.m. from Gold Digger, "Hello ma frenn," she sang.

"What's up?" *And why the hell are you calling me right now?*

"Guess what?" she chirped.

"What?" *Betch, I ain't playing these games right now.*

"[Gay Porn Star] thinks he left his phone in your car last night."

I stayed silent. *You're all idiots, I swear.*

"I need you to meet us at the hotel."[117]

"Uh, are you sure he left it in my car?" I asked in disbelief.

"Yes, he ran 'Find my iPhone' and the address is your house."

"Whyyy?! What kind of drunk are you dating?" I moaned.

"I know, he's so dumb sometimes. He irritates me."

Says the two-timing ho. He deserves someone better than your gold digging ass.

"I'll send you the address. We can go to lunch." Her words were giving me a headache.

"No, it's cool. I'll just swing it by."

"Okayyy ma fren. See you soon." *Click.*

All I wanted to do was to be done with these people. They were and are so twisted, constantly intertwined in a gigantic orgy (some knowingly participate, while others are clueless). So, I was in no rush to bring a phone and decided to carry my morning out as I usually would on a Sunday.

Around 10:30 a.m., I left my house to bring the cursed iPhone to the hotel. I was so close to a clean getaway, but Gold Digger just had to throw some twisted loop into my escape plan.

She greeted me with an overly zealous, "Oh yeah! You're here!"

I hugged her and then slid past her as I handed the phone to GPS (acronym for Gay Porn Star). "Here's the phone...Be more careful, you crazy drunk!" I fake punched his shoulder.

Gay Porn Star laughed and thanked me, and we all could've left it at that, but *of course* Gold Digger had to get another dig in, "So we're going to lunch with [El Tramposo]. Come on, we're going to his villa now."

Bitch. She is doing this on purpose. She knows.

I couldn't say no. Everyone else would've suspected something was up. I tried to make it sound like I was already committed to something

---

[117] El Tramposo decided to get two ridiculously priced villas at Pelican Hill. One for him and Unicorn and the other for Gold Digger, since GD had thrown a fit... They were obviously still fucking.

else, but she knew I was lying and I was too concerned with the way everyone else would view me if they, too, knew I was lying. I could've spared myself so much embarrassment had I just left, but I agreed to go like a naive idiot, thinking that this was the better of the two options. Hindsight is always 20/20.

GD, GPS and I all went in my car while the office gays and the other company partner went in another car. We arrived at El Tramposo's villa (which was of course much bigger and better than the other villa), coincidentally just in time to watch Unicorn walk down the stairs with dirty sex hair.[118] I was so tempted to compliment her on her gloriously greasy sex hair—"Someone fucked you sloppy"—but alas, I refused and took a higher road, after all, it wasn't her fault El Tramposo was such a pig. I refused to look at him which was proving to be highly effective tactic. There were too many people there to realize that two of us weren't talking (or that one of us was refusing to acknowledge the other).

The group wrapped it up at his ostentatious villa, and we piled into two cars to Yard House. (Yes. Back to the Yard House. Are you starting to see that Yard House is a horrible place for me?) I drove one car with the office gays and Gay Porn Star while El Tramposo drove the car with his two bimbos (aka Unicorn and Gold Digger) and the other partner and his girlfriend. As El Tramposo backed out of his parking space, he nearly knocked my German-tank-of-a-car with his stupid American Hemi engine truck. I took this as a challenge: he wanted to race me.

Everyone just thought we were racing for the fun of getting to lunch first, but I knew, and he knew, that we were competing to prove who had a bigger dick (I say that as a figure of speech) and, even more so, as a show of how unaffected we were by the other's actions. Yeah, I know it sounds preposterous, but I had to WIN! Oh, and did I win! I smoked his ass. We got to dreadful Yard House and waited ten minutes for El Tramposo and his bimbo buggy.

---

[118] We later found out at lunch that she never washed or blow dried her own hair. She paid a dry bar to do that at least once a week; hence, her extra nasty hair that morning.

Have I mentioned how much I despise Yard House? The hostess sat us at a table for nine people. Everyone was coupled off, except for me of course. That being so, all of the couples sat together, and I had to sit in between two couples. Guess where I sat?! If you guessed right next to El Tramposo and directly across from Unicorn, then you guessed right. I sat on the far end of the table first, thinking El Tramposo got the hint that I didn't want to talk to him, let alone be near him but apparently he hadn't a clue. Being the pompous social retard he is, El Tramposo sat right next to me at the head of the table. *Ooo, wunderbar!* And of course, he had to spread out his legs to "accidentally" graze mine while he rubbed Unicorn's leg under the table in plain sight. Her Majesty, Unicorn, sat right smack across from me, making sure to put her precious baby of an Alexander McQueen purse hanging off of the back of her chair. It was for all to see as she mentioned multiple times how ET[119] bought it for her as an early Christmas gift. *Gag.*

Seeing as the purse was a big, boxy bag and the restaurant was slamming busy with tight walkways between tables, it was obvious to me that her damn suitcase was in the way for servers as they walked through carrying trays full of food and drinks. And when the inevitable happened, and they knocked it off of her chair, she threw a fit. Unicorn just couldn't wrap her twatty, southern twanging head around the fact that that stupid bag was in the way! I wanted to tell her to shut up, and came close to it, but silenced myself when I remembered I did not want to make a scene.

Poor thing, you could see the cluelessness in her eyes, the vacancy in her brain and the shallow love in her heart. Regardless of her lack of common sense, she managed to entertain the table for nearly the whole of lunch. And other than the purse catastrophe and a skull-draining abundance of y'all's, everyone and everything got along smoothly.

That is until Unicorn announced to the table how wonderful the chocolate chip s'mores cookies were in ET's fridge, "Oh my goodness, y'all, I ate so many cookies yesterday!"[120]

---

[119] Alien freak.
[120] Insert obnoxious twang here.

146

Oh fuck.

Gold Digger orgasmically rolled her eyes back in her head, earnestly concerning herself, "Mmmm really? Where? I want some cookies."

"I ate them at [ET's] house. They were so tasty. I couldn't stop eating them."[121]

"Nom nom nom...what kind?" GD said all giddy. (Yes she seriously talks like this—but then again so do I—must be why we were friends.)

Just then, ET the super-genius answered and pointed to me, "Oh, Dax made them for me."

Gold Digger looked at him as though he was referring to his ex-mistress, the one who also has the same name as mine, but El Tramposo quickly clarified that by nodding his head toward me and saying, "This Dax."

Silence.

DIE!!!! YOU IDIOT!

Silence.

Silence.

Silence.

Everyone awkwardly stared at him and then me. It was so quiet you could almost hear Unicorn's brain explode...*Mind blown.*

Seconds were screaming by as I struggled to find cover from the revelation now hanging over our table. *Oh, god. Oh, god. Think. Think. What the hell. Stupid idiot! Stab him with your butter knife. No. That's too obvious. Too many witnesses. Focus. Thinkkkkkk.*

Ah! Finally, I found the words I had been searching for, "Ah, those cookies...the s'more chippers? Yeah, those are a family tradition. We always give them out to friends. I made them for [El Tramposo] (what I meant to say was Satan) and his kids."

Damn cookies ruined everything. At this point, everybody fuckin' knew. They could see the panic in my eyes and hear the hatred in my voice. All the while, El Tramposo sat back relaxed, watching my brain unravel as I tried to cover up our embarrassingly tainted relation. I swear that bastard did it on purpose. It was like he wanted Unicorn to know.

---

[121] Ooh, looks like you could insert that twang again...y'all!

As though he had gotten some sick pleasure from that. I know he said it on purpose.

Luckily we had nearly finished lunch because the tension was almost unbearable. Unicorn wouldn't look at me and ironically directed all of her attention toward Gold Digger (who, at this point, I was sure was still fucking El Tramposo too. After all, he was paying for her overpriced apartment that she couldn't have afforded otherwise.). I was so ashamed. I had already processed the fact that he was a cheater and hadn't changed and probably never would. I was one of at least four other women (two of which were named my godawful real name), and I felt disgusting.

And, in some weird, twisted way, I almost felt responsible for the fate of Unicorn, but how was I supposed to know that he was with so many girls? He had sworn off women the first time we met for a drink, and I had sworn off men after my experience with Dane. I was devastated, but at least I had the privacy of discovering the truth at a bustling party where no one else knew what was going on. Poor Unicorn. She had it worse. I cannot fathom how this simpleminded southern woman felt when she discovered that her stallion of a man was nothing more than an ass. To add to the drama, her earth was shattered in front of a table of people who were nearly strangers to her.

The check was paid, goodbyes were said, and paths were parted. But once again, my clean getaway was obstructed. El Tramposo decided it would be appropriate to send me nasty text messages, faulting me for his cheating ways.[122] At first, El Tramposo's texts blamed me for his behavior. After about twenty of those, and still no response from me, he decided to change his tone and began to apologize and ask for me back. I kid you not! That motherfucker went from crazy to crazier in a matter of minutes.[123] I eventually responded. Being as cruelly sincere as I could be, I told him he was disgusting and that he was retarded if he thought I was going to ever speak to him again after that shit show. Then I blocked his number and never spoke to him again.

---

[122] I'm still confused by this.
[123] See, I told you that ignoring men usually works!

BZZ BZZ BULLSHIT

●● ● ●●

"I'm doing to her, what you did to me!"
Um okay, aggressive.

●● ● ●●

Ahh, the wonderments of dating through an app. This is seriously what a world looking for love has come to: a virtual dating drive-thru. No one my age meets organically anymore. Every single under-thirty friend that I have uses Tinder or Bumble or Hinge, but I was always the holdout. I refused. Why would I want to enlist myself into another dating war zone? I mean, *free* online dating services? No good could come from that. Nothing worthwhile is ever free.

I had heard horror stories of men using services like these to discreetly cheat on their wives or longtime girlfriends (and I think we can all agree that I had enough of that to last me a lifetime), and of course I had heard all about the swinging couples who use these as a platform to add persons to their lovesome. As far as I was concerned, the app dating trail was dusted with only a few tall tales of finding true love. Besides, I didn't need the help of an app to get a date. I get asked out all of the time. *By who? Who the hell asks you out?* Okay, so maybe I don't get asked out all of the time.

It had been about four months since I had rid myself of my last cheater and I guess you could say I was getting "cabin fever."[124] My two best friends were both traveling a lot for work and gay adventures, and besides the two of them, I didn't associate myself with anyone...

---

[124] No, I do not literally mean I live in a cabin. It's a figure of speech, meaning that I was getting mother fucking antsy.

at least, not willingly. I mean I hung out with my mom. Yup, I would have rather stayed at home with my mom than go out with people my own age that I didn't like all that much.[125] But living a double life as a twenty-three-year-old woman and an almost-fifty-year-old woman was wearing.

I mean, I would wake up anywhere between 5:45 and 10:00 a.m. (depending on how committed I was to being skinny). I would then force myself to go on a hike with my bastard son (a.k.a. Igor Schnitzel VonFrankenstein, my furry shelter baby). Then I'd drive twenty minutes away from home to go to my favorite coffee shop to write for my acting class, and later, between 12:00 and 1:30 p.m., I'd persuade myself into doing some hot yoga. After that, I'd hit up Whole Foods for a pineapple-ginger juice (which they recently discontinued from the juice bar and that pisses me off) and then return home in time to vicariously live out the rest of my day as a middle-aged single mother of three. Do you see how exhausting that is? Don't get me wrong: I learned a lot about primetime television and menopause...both are shit.

I was *EXHAUSTED*. My schedule was jam-packed with a whole lot of nothing, and I was making it seem as though that was enough to fill the whole of my life. With Adler technique classes on Mondays from 7:00 to 10:00 p.m. and work on Friday and Saturday nights from 4:00 p.m. to maybe 12:30 a.m., if I had to close the restaurant.[126] Life was complicated. I couldn't bother myself with any more little boys—my promising acting career was about to take off any day now. I could feel it in my bones![127]

Needless to say, I was starting to grow restless (and really fucking bored) in the little game called life I had been playing. I needed some *zsa zsa zsu*.[128] (Oooh, sounds exotic.) But where the hell was I supposed to find that?

---

[125] Very Important Side Note: I still do that.

[126] Oh yeah, sorry I don't actually get paid for my acting work besides my unfeatured background work.

[127] Note: I'm still waiting for this career to take off...any day now...any day.

[128] Yes, I am making a *Sex and the City* reference.

I had been considering the online dating scene for some time, but I still had not been wholly convinced by the pop-up pictures of hotties they showed on the app description in the iTunes store. To make matters even more pathetic, I had done extensive research on the subject: What online profiles draw the most traffic? How to write an alluring bio. How to pick pictures for your desired audience. I already knew how to ham it up in person, but I also knew none of that would matter if my profile didn't hook the big fish I wanted.

So after a few TED Talks on building an online dating profile and "Questions to Fall in Love," as well as a couple of psychology articles and a sprinkling of the knowledge I had gained from my best straight guy friend, I armed myself for yet another battle to find love. *God, here we go again.*

I downloaded the app—you know, the one that's yellow and goes buzz buzz. The entire time it was loading onto my phone, I kept thinking about going back. I was scared of this tiny, virtual world that I had never stepped into before. *I don't want to do this. I really shouldn't be doing this. I don't think I'm ready for this.* The app loaded, and the welcome screen popped up, inviting me to create a profile. I thought about everything I had read and watched and asked and learned. *Okay, I'm ready.*

I began to hack away at my stupid iPhone, flipping through pictures that I found to showcase me—not too much makeup but not ugly ass either. I chose five photos, purposefully placing both a dressed up and goofy picture in the mix with three standard everyday looks. Then I started to brainstorm my bio. I remembered from one TED Talk (yes, I am serious about this) that the profiles that receive the most "traffic" are the ones with simple and to-the-point bios. If you don't have a bio, then you may be deterring viable suitors (which makes it sound like I'm looking for a sperm donor), and if your bio is too complicated then by default, you're too complicated. My bio was straightforward, a little cliché (seeing as every hoochie within a one-hundred-mile radius of me LOVES coffee, yoga and the great outdoors)[129] and one giant incomplete, run-on sentence—Hey! Just like my book! Perhaps I put

---

[129] Coffee, yoga and the great outdoors…it's just like so effin' Southern Californian.

too much thought into it, but I figured if I was going to do something like that, then I would at least do it "right."

My profile was complete and I began swiping away. Left was no and right was yes. Easy enough, right? Initially I had to keep reminding myself which was yes and which was no, but soon it became muscle memory. At first, I took careful consideration of every profile that I came across. I was trying to be realistic and mature in my eligible bachelors as I binge watched *American Horror Story* on Netflix. I read every one of their profiles, flipped through all of their pictures and tried to imagine how they were in real life. I hadn't written anything misleading about myself on my profile and I sure as hell hadn't filtered the shit out of any of my pictures and I held these complete strangers to the same standard. Some were cute, some were ehhhh, and some were BABESSSSS. *Maybe this stupid online thing won't be so bad?* I felt like I was winning every time I got a new match...I was so proud of myself for creating such a kickass profile.

Would you like for me to bring my pathetic game to a whole new level? Okay ladies, here you go...I had even pulled three questions from the "Questions to Fall in Love" article that I found to be thought-provoking:

Given the choice of anyone in the world, whom would you want as a dinner guest?

If you were able to live to the age of ninety, would you rather retain the mind or body of a thirty-year-old?

If you could wake up tomorrow having gained any one quality or ability, what would it be?

I would sort through the eligibility pool by their answers to my questions. I had grading scale criteria on which I would then base my decision:

A.) They don't respond at all,

B.) They respond but don't consider my question and don't ask me anything,

C.) They considered my question and answered, and

D.) They considered my question and answered and asked me a question in response.

If they graded a C or D, then I would respond, but A's and B's got deleted from my dating pool, no matter how hot they were. It was so simple and oh-so empowering to be able to go through men like that—although it did, unfortunately, eliminate quite a few hotties. To keep it fun, I tried to show some self-restraint by only permitting myself to buzz the bullshit at night and never out in public. It took just about a week for me to get asked out on my first buzzing date and, oh lordy, was I one excited hoochie mama. Little did I know that I was about to discover several lessons along the way about the new world that I had entered…Oh, the perils of online dating.

...

It was late one night whilst exploring the buzzer when we matched. *Ding.* He seemed cute, active and mature. Immediately, I sent him one of the prepared questions that I ripped off from the "Questions to Fall in Love" article: "If you could live until you were ninety years old, would you rather retain the body or mentality of a thirty-year-old?"

He promptly responded, "I'd rather maintain the body of a thirty-year-old and have the wisdom of a ninety-year-old who has lived and loved through a lost world." I couldn't help but fall in love with his answer. He also mentioned that he was impressed by my question and who was I to tell him that I had pulled it from a TED Talk? So I accepted his compliment and the conversation carried on through that pesky little yellow app.

After about ten messages back and forth, he asked me for my phone number which I gladly listed out for him. Our conversation propelled us into the early morning until it was finally he that ended the banter with a good night. I was so excited. He was the first man to keep a meaningful/thought-provoking conversation going on that damn dating app.

The following day he invited me to grab a drink with him a little later that week. We decided on a bar not too far from either one of our houses, and I had to wait a whole two days before I got to meet eligible bachelor number one in person. The day couldn't have come any quicker, and I had decided to ease the pain of my nerves by meeting up with the biggest playboy I knew...my best friend, Rambo. (Loves ya, kid!)

Rambo and I met for a drink down the street with his brother and a couple of their friends. I told him I had a date and, of course, he mocked me since I had to tell him that I had met this fella though Bumble. Shall I put it all in perspective for you? I have always told him those dating apps were disgusting and that I would never use them since that's how Rambo had gotten all of his girls. It was no wonder that he made fun of me.

"Don't waste your time meeting up with this loser," Rambo interjected.

"Says the King of Tinder," I jested back.

"No, seriously, this guy is going to be a joke."

I laughed in Rambo's face.

"There's probably something wrong with him," he tried to reason.

"Be honest, the only reason you want me here is so that you can hit on more girls. You need me to be your wingwoman—Admit it!"

"Well, yeah. Dax, don't leave me with these losers," he joked, nodding his head toward all of his friends.

"No thank you," I said slamming my drink down. Rambo wasn't going to be right or at least that's what my stubborn self thought.

I drove to the bar, waved at the doorman who's always there, and sat against the giant art installation wall. Texting the man that I was soon about to know more about than I wanted to. I told him where he could find me in the bar. Five minutes passed and in he walked, tall and not exactly like his pictures. Yeah, he lied. *Fuck, Rambo was right. Damn it. Whatever, be cool.* He was cute, but in his pics he looked smoking hot. (I guess that's lesson one of online dating: no one is ever as hot as their pictures.)

Not only was he physically different, he was a completely different being in person. Maybe he was nervous, or maybe I wasn't what he had perceived me to be from my profile either. He wasn't as well-spoken as he had been through text and he was difficult to understand over the thudding beat of the electronic mix in the bar. He didn't ask me anything meaningful, but he did leave me with a lot of useful tidbits of information about himself. For example, he was in the midst of a divorce. That's a significant bit of information to withhold from someone because of what it brings to the proverbial "table."

It wasn't that he was in the middle of a divorce that bothered me; it was that it was all he could talk about during our so-called "date." I didn't care that he had to sell his business or that his wife had just decided one day after seven years that she didn't want to be with him and left...I mean my heart went out to him, but why would I go on a date to hear about someone else's problems? I was sorry that he seemed to be a great, if not broken guy—but I couldn't be his therapist.

I sipped on my drink while Almost-Divorcee pounded three. I considered getting hammered drunk just to entertain myself but quickly decided against it. I didn't want to get drunk with this sad and lost man. What I wanted to do was get rip-roaring drunk with Rambo, who I should have listened to when he told me to bail on this date. So Almost-Divorcee and I finished our spirits, and we left.

Almost-Divorcee walked me to my car and hugged me goodbye, a big strong hug that whispered his soul's sadness. "I'll talk to you soon," he said as he turned away to his oversized gas-guzzling truck.

"Yeah, cool," I replied knowing that we would never speak again.

And just like that, my first Bumble date was over. Painfully awkward, but I was still alive and kicking. I dipped my fat toe in the water and learned that it was unpredictable and sometimes a bit chilly but that I could withstand it if I wanted to. At the very least, these guys would make for a great story (hopefully) or maybe some friends to add to the plethora of friends that I already had (or don't have). Almost-Divorcee was a not-so-successful start to a two-month journey of surfing the Bumble dating app world. Though in hindsight, he was one of the more "normal" ones.

...

Two weeks into the damn dating app and I was already an addict. For someone like me who loves to keep her mind busy with tons of multitasking, I loved that little tempestuous devil of an app. I was clearly no longer following my rule of not Bumble-ing in public spaces. I could have five different conversations going on through the app's messaging and texting—and, oh my god, was it fun! The best part was that I would never save their numbers in my phone so I had to be on my toes at all times and remember certain details about each guy. I guess this was my new favorite game.

My grading scale of elimination was quite useful in weeding out the duds. My range now had a new level on top of the previously established one: If they asked for my phone number, I would give it to them. If they asked for my phone number and then a date, I would accept. If they asked for my number and we spoke for a few days, but they never asked me out, then I would stop responding to them and delete their contact info from my messaging so as to not mistake them for a more eligible bachelor. As you can see, this was all very scientific, and I suppose I wasn't taking anything too seriously. But I was having fun.

After my first date, I concluded that there was probably a profusion of men just like Almost-Divorcee on this app. Not necessarily men who were in the midst of a divorce but most definitely some sad and lost boys. I was wary of them. I didn't need any more of that in my life; I was just learning what it meant to take charge and do what I wanted to do. There was no way I would allow myself to be brought down again by some sad soul. I had big, scheming plans to be a bit of a player...at least for a couple of months.

One night, while (not) watching T.V. and swiping through all of the contenders, I came across Millionaire Fuckboy. Of course, that wasn't his real name, and his profile didn't mention anything about money. There was a picture of him with his mom, a picture with his dad, a picture of him playing basketball, and a full body (clothed)[130] selfie. He was cute and what he had written for himself was endearingly uncomplicated. Basically he stated that hard work prevailed over all and how much he loved his family...Swipe right. We matched immediately, so I sent him the message that I had copied onto every guy's introductory message: "Given anyone in the world, who would you want as a dinner guest?" The message sent and I exited out of the app and went to bed.

The following afternoon, I was on my way to L.A. for an audition (I didn't get it, the part, in case you were wondering...surprise, surprise) when I got stuck in traffic on the 110 freeway through Downtown. I determined, what better time to check my Bumble but now...in traffic. So I opened that pesky bugger of an app and saw that I had some notifications—one of them being a reply from Millionaire Fuckboy. *Woot woot!* He responded to my question and asked me the question back.

He was already winning in my book. We bantered back and forth a bit—by which I mean like two message exchanges each—and then he asked me for my number almost immediately. *Whoa, mama likes herself a straightforward man!* Our conversation seemed never-ending, carrying on for days on end. The best part about him was that he wanted to go out with me right away, so we made plans for that Thursday night.

MF had warned me that Thursday nights were boys' nights but that he would love for me to come and meet all of his friends. I thought he was amazing and we hadn't even met in person yet. I found his upfront personality admirable. I was going to meet him at The Bungalow in Santa Monica. (Talk about boojee.) I left my house and headed there after traffic died, arriving sometime around 9:00 p.m. The area was a mess with construction and drunk idiots walking everywhere. I valeted because I was too impatient to look for parking. Fixing my tight grey dress that kept riding up, I grabbed my (faux) leather jacket and tossed

---

[130] Any guys reading this? Please stop putting ab and close-to-dick pics on social media...at this point we all know that you're butter faces. Thank you.

my keys to the valet. *Fuck I'm nervous.* I called Mr. Fuckboy, "Hey, where you at?"

"Hey, what's up…We're under the big tree just past the entrance."

"Cool, I'm here. Oh, wait I see you." *Click.*

I walked up to MF and his friend, hellos and hugs were exchanged, and then the three of us headed to the bar for Don Julio and pineapples all around. I could tell he was nervous too, which was a relief considering how nervous I had been walking through the entrance. His friend was the happy mediator between the two of us, distracting us from our debilitating butterflies.

Once the alcohol began to settle in our bellies, the night started to take off. We were having a blast and, after about an hour or two at The Bungalow, MF suggested that we leave for someplace better. "Anywhere you want to go, I can get us in anywhere," he said, assuring me that the night was mine to take.

I still hadn't a clue of who he was or what he did. I just thought he knew a lot of people. "You can be my guide. I trust you," I said not knowing the area too well and not being one for the nightclub scene.

In complete unison, he and his friend looked at each other and said, "Hyde."

"Where's that?" I asked them.

"It's in Hollywood," MF informed me.

"I can drive," I offered.

"Where's your car at?" the friend asked.

"Oh, I valeted."

"I'll pay for it," said MF.

"Why? I can pay for it."

"Oh please, you know who you came out with," sneered his friend.

"We're going to get an Uber. You don't need to drive," MF benevolently dictated. So, he called us an Uber and off we went, leaving my car behind.

We arrived at Hyde and, on first impression, the place didn't seem that great. It wasn't even busy, but for some reason, the bouncers at the door weren't letting people inside. Millionaire Fuckboy grabbed my hand, skipping us past some people and walked us right up to the front of the line. The friend dipped out and told us he'd be back but he had to get his lady who lived down the street.

"Hey man, the name's [MF]."

"We're full, buddy," snapped the cheaply dressed bouncer.

"Call Miguel. You want to let me in."

Then someone from the staff walked up and whispered something into the bouncer's ear. They stared back at us, and MF looked like he meant business.

"Oh, yeah, hey man, how ya doing? Come on in." the bouncer said quickly changing his hard tone.

"Thanks man, my homie just went to grab his girl. Let him in when he gets back," MF nodded while taking me by the hand, leading me past the bouncer.

In we walked, MF knew where he was going, taking my hand and weaving me through the crowd of insanely dressed beautiful bodies. I probably looked starstruck. I didn't know who this kid was. He was just two years older than me, and he had the whole front staff of this inflated club eating out of his hand. MF led me to the bar, grabbed us another round of Don Julio and pineapples and posted up against the countertop. We chatted for a bit, each being more comfortable with the other. He told me things that he "never" told anyone,[131] and I listened in awe.

His compadre came back womanless and on the prowl for some drinks and some ladies. We had a drink or more and then headed out onto the dance floor. The friend had some other friends with a table so we made our way to them.

"Do you want a table?" MF whispered to me.

"Uh, I don't think you should waste your money on a table," I replied, uncomfortable with the superfluous amount of money he was offering to spend.

---

[131] He would always preface something from his youth with "I've never told anyone this," or close his remark with, "Wow, I can't believe I just told you that. I've never said that to anyone." But truth be told, he would tell anyone and everyone everything about him when he was blacked-out drunk which was at least three times a week.

"If you want it, I'll get it for you."

"No, I don't need a table. Let's save it for another night."

He kissed my cheek, "You're the coolest girl I've met." I quizzically looked at him, not understanding why I was so cool but he continued, "No girl has ever told me not to get a table. Usually their eyes bug out at the thought of it." He snickered probably thinking about a specific girl or two, I'm sure.

The night carried on, and our dancing cascaded us through nearly the whole of it. The two amigos were sloshed drunk, and I was happy with my buzz (which means I was piss drunk). Rap music was pounding, pulsing through our hips in a primal fashion. MF courted me on the dance floor, while his confidant ran around the club looking for new girls to scheme on. *Boom, boom, boom,* our bodies bounced with the bounty of new relations. His arms around my waist, he planted another kiss on my face. I was in a pure drunken state. The friend rolled back in, "Let's go, man. This is whack." So MF called for another Uber Deluxe and off we went, back to the Westside.

The next morning I awoke to an alarm chirping. I didn't budge, the bed was warm and the room was dark and silent. Again, a chirping filled my hibernating eardrums, and again, the bedroom remained lifeless. More time passed and then, "Oh shit!" Millionaire Fuckboy sprung out of his bed, leaving me fully dressed and completely cuddled in his sheets. "Damn it. I'm going to be so late for work. I'm so sorry. You can stay here as long as you want, but I have to go." With that, MF jumped into a pair of pants he had jumbled up on the floor in a monstrous pile of clothing. He ran back over to the bed and kissed me goodbye. No sooner than I heard the door click did I call an Uber to get my car from The Bungalow.

In an effort to gain more brownie points with MF, I thought it wise and oh-so sweet to bring him breakfast and coffee to his office which was just across the freeway (but because it was L.A., it still took me an hour and a half to get it to him). I texted him offering him something, already knowing what his answer would be. He was ecstatic with joy. I knew that I had him exactly where I wanted him. I paraded into his office building, to the top floor where I flashed him with my good graces and the equivalent of crack cocaine to a hungover man-boy...a breakfast burrito and a giant iced vanilla latte with extra shots of espresso. He may have been able to work a club, but I knew how to work a boy.

I sat with Fuckboy in the office awhile where he purposely had me watch him do "business." He talked about money and used the jargon of a seasoned partner. I'm not going to lie—it was kind of hot that he was so confident in what he did. He thanked me a million times, walked me out of the office and kissed me goodbye. Our future was set. Even though I still wasn't sure exactly who this kid was, but I knew that I liked his simple roots and I admired what he achieved through hard work.

We had met through Bumble because MF had been in my Bumble radius looking at houses since his company was expanding down to O.C. He still had a couple of weeks left in L.A. before he made his move down to my neck of the woods. What that meant is that we still had plenty of time to go out and play in the City of Angels.

So, no more than a week after our first meeting, MF invited me out for his roommate's birthday party. We had been talking nonstop, and I think every girl will agree with me that when a guy invites you to his friend's birthday or anything involving his friends, it is a BIG deal.[132] The six of us headed to some club in Downtown. At first, it was lame. All we had access to was this overcrowded bar that was filled to the brim with obnoxious college students trying to be big league in Downtown L.A. When MF decided that he was over it, he went to some secret door that looked like a wall and told the doorman something to get us in.

We passed through a wall into another dimension. In this world, there was a HUGE dance floor and a giant stage with a DJ playing all of the best rap and electronic mixes. I looked at Millionaire Fuckboy through my drunken stupor and thought, *You're amazing*. This man-boy had just transported us into an Alice-in-Wonderland-type world... going through one door into an entirely different world that I would've never known existed. We danced and danced and danced, and then

---

[132] So that means that I'm kind of like a big deal...right?

when the music stopped, and the bodies started rolling out, we snuck away and headed back to his home.

Although that was only my second time hanging out with him in person, I was starting to learn something: when he drank, he got a little too loose with his money. Blacked-out Millionaire Fuckboy was also a total bragger, which was annoying. I wasn't hanging out with him for his money, I was hanging out with him because I loved how candidly he had spoken to me about his not so easy upbringing and how humble he had appeared to be and how high he set his standards and goals. I didn't care about his money. Ever.

This was the night that he decided it to be "cool" to tell me how much money he spent at Hyde: "Yeah, I dropped like forty grand there the other night. That's why they let me do whatever I want." I shushed him and prayed that the Uber driver wasn't listening to his shallow words. MF laughed at me for telling him that money didn't matter, "You're great." *Yeah, I know I'm great, but stop talking about how much money you have in front of complete strangers.* I still wasn't aware of how much money this naive little boy had at his dispersion.

Then came the big day: MF's move to Orange County. I was starting to get annoyed with him, not because he was obnoxious but because we still hadn't gone out on a date just the two of us. Like some idiots before him, he used the excuse that he was "super busy with work." *And I'm like SUPER busy being a drama queen.* So I got a little impatient and decided to grab the bull by the horns and accept a date from a guy that I had already been talking to on Bumble. To be fair, I had agreed to meet this guy before I started talking to MF, but he was studying for his doctor boards and was also going back to the midwest to visit his mom and dad. So our long-awaited date was very much anticipated.

Millionaire Fuckboy had been in Orange County for barely a week and had moved into one of the most coveted areas but was too embarrassed to have me over to his house because he said it was small and shitty.[133] And sorry (not sorry), I was not going to wait for him to get his head out of his ass. So on to Doc I went.

Doc was handsome with a capital H-A-N-D-S-O-M-E. He had black hair and bright blue eyes and the sweetest demeanor. He was from Illinois so he had that humble, midwest vibe. Golly, he was adorable... he made me not want to say bad words in front of him. (Mom, look what a respectable lady I've become.)[134]

Doc set our date for drinks at a popping Mexican restaurant. Typical me, I got there way too early. I parked my car, texted Doc to tell him where I was in the bar, and posted up against the wall in the only free space available. I could feel the butterflies tickling the lining of my stomach as I waited for him. *I wonder what he'll be like. I hope I'm not taller than him.*[135] Then I saw him, the sea of people parted and everyone everywhere got quiet.

"Hey, Dax?"

"Hi, [Doc]."

He embraced me in a tight and worthy hug. "You look beautiful," he commented, making me blush. He was even cuter in person than he was on his profile. We walked to the bar where he ordered himself a Modelo Especial and a margarita for me (I didn't want him to know how fucked up beer made me, so I stuck with the tequila...you know, my best friend).

The hours quickly passed. Doc was by far the best date I had been on. He was so knowledgeable yet so down to earth, and I was truly enjoying myself.

The bar began to clear out, but we still had plenty of time before closing, both of us had been nursing the same drink for two hours. When Doc got up to go to the restroom, I checked my phone. I had one missed call and a flurry of text messages from MF (of course I did). I swear guys like him have an insecure sensor implanted in their bodies

---

[133] With all the damn money that that boy had, I don't know why he didn't buy himself a house? Mind-blowing.

[134] Yeah fucking right.

[135] I had been on two other Bumble dates (that aren't worthy of talking about) and learned that I was taller than both men...no big deal, I guess.

that zaps 'em when you're on a date. His messages loaded up in a long stream that just kept going and going:

"Hey, what's up?"

"Want to go out?"

"I just finished work."

"We're going to head to L.A."

"You should come with."

"When my boss and I go out, we go big."

"I want you to meet him."

"Hello?"

"Are you out on a date?"

"If you are, you can tell me."

"I swear I won't get mad. I'm not even jealous."

I started scanning through the bar area of the restaurant, wondering if Millionaire Fuckboy was there. *Nope, no sign of him.* So I replied to his pathetic string of incessant messages: "Bahaha no, I'm not on a date. I'm grabbing a drink with my friend, but we're almost done. What time are you leaving?" *Dax, you sellout.*

Doc returned from the bathroom with a giant smile on his face. I smirked back knowing that I wanted to wrap it up to go out to L.A. for what was guaranteed to be a night to remember. He probably sensed my rush and asked me if it was time to go, I smiled and said "Yeah, I told my friends that I would meet up with them to go out to L.A. tonight." (I am so dumb.) He looked disappointed but smiled anyway.

"Okay, let's go," he said.

He walked me to my car where an awkward little dance ensued. You know, that one when you're not sure if it's appropriate for you to kiss. He hugged me again, tightly. He was so cute. I got into my car; he shut the door and walked himself back to the valet to get his car. I waved goodbye as I geared my car toward MF's house.

I pushed the thought of Doc back in my mind to avoid the inevitable guilt I felt by giving this awesome guy the "go-around" as I dialed MF's number. He answered, and I already knew he was close to blacked-out drunk, if not already blacked-out drunk. *Great, now he's going to give me the go-around.* Instantaneously, I regretted leaving Doc behind to pursue a man that was slowly becoming more broken to me.

"Hey, I'm heading down south now. I'll be there in ten."

"Ah man, we already left!"

"No, you didn't," I seethed.

"Yeah we did. We're going to the strip club. The boss man loves that shit."

"Well, hold the car," I politely suggested. (It was more of a command than a suggestion.)

"We're almost to Hollywood. HAAA, guess what kind of car we have?!"

"What?" I insincerely asked because I sincerely did not care.

"I got us a Rolls!"

I was waiting for the reggae horns to trumpet in the background as he told me...you know those ones in rap songs and on hip hop stations.

"Hmm, so cool." I didn't give a fuck about an old man car.

"We're so pimpin' right now." He was stoked.

"Yeah, you're such a pimp. I'm going home."

"No, come out. Just drive to Hollywood."

"No. I don't want to leave my car overnight."

"Get an Uber..."

"I'm not paying for an Uber when there's only an hour before closing time."

"Whatever, you're missing out."

"Night," I hung up.

I drove myself home, fueling my drive with the moments of the date and pondering why I had ended it early when I knew that MF was nothing but a child lost in his money. Laying myself in bed, I checked my phone to find a text from Doc. He thanked me for the wonderful evening we had and wanted to take me out again. Thinking of the dead-end MF was coming to, I told him that I couldn't wait. We continued blowing each other's phones up until I fell asleep, but my phone continued to dance through the early morning as MF texted me sweet nothings about his annual salary. (See, that's when I knew he was blacked-out.)

My and Fuckboy's time was coming to an end. I wasn't going to wait around for some kid who couldn't drink without getting blacked-out and with whom I'd have to worry about telling everyone in the bar how much money he had (that's a sure way to get jumped). I continued speaking to Doc but seeing as he was busy studying for his boards and swamped with his orthopedic internship, we didn't have much time to spend with each other. I wasn't rushing in to find a boyfriend or a husband, but I knew that I didn't want a "friend with benefits" or a fuck buddy or any of those immature and insecure things. I wanted to start working on building an honest relationship with someone and start exploring the world (I'm serious here). MF had potential but was insecure without his money, and Doc had tons of potential only he was too busy and would be moving across the country soon if he got accepted into the surgical residency he wanted. That left me with one option...I had to continue buzzing through Bumble to find new matches with new potential. Do you think I was addicted?

...

Millionaire Fuckboy and I hadn't hung out in a couple of weeks, but I didn't mind, I wasn't taking him seriously and had been the one to tell him that I thought we would be better friends than lovers (seeing as he wasn't too loving when he was sober). He respected my suggestion, and we mutually agreed to friendship (by mutually, I mean just me). So I kept swiping away, continuing my copy-and-paste question spree.

I was starting to get fed up with the whole Bumble thing; it was so easy, yet so complicated. All of the guys I was meeting were great in their own way, but so far none of them were long-term-relationship-types of guys. I became more lackadaisical in my approach; I had to—the damn thing started running out of men in the meat market for me. Swiping right became my new best friend...I figured I should expand my horizons and expanding my horizons led me straight to a new type of guy. Meet Too Hip to Function.

Too Hip to Function was the type of guy that was somehow good at every form of art. He knew all about all sorts of literature and pieces of art and ways of thinking. He was pensive, yet grounded; thoughtful, yet careless; intelligent, yet naive; and giving, yet selfish. To me, he was a walking oxymoron. There were so many wonderful bits about him, but also so much that I could never appreciate. We had a lot in common and nothing in common, and we definitely weren't meant to be.

THTF answered my infamous icebreaking question in a completely different and attention-grabbing fashion to me. He responded by telling me, "Depends on whether or not I would still be loved and if I still had people that made me happy because if I didn't then, I wouldn't want to live until I was ninety." His reply boggled my mind and left me speechless; no one in the two months I had been on Bumble had ever been that creative and honest sounding in their response. *Hmmm, how peculiar.* We chitchatted back and forth, and then he made my favorite Bumble boy move: he asked me for my phone number. *Holla!* It wasn't long before he asked me on a date. *Weeeeeeee.*

We met for coffee, although he drank green tea because his herbalist (yes, his herbalist) told him that it was better for his particular metabolism. When we got to the counter, I did the test. You know, the test—the one where you act like you're going to pay and then the guy should step in and pay. THTF failed…BIG time.

I'm all for being an independent and self-sufficient woman (because I am one), but I'm also all about the tradition of a guy paying on the date that he asked me out on…especially the first date. Had it been the reverse, then I would have paid. Despite his little hiccup in payment, our date was a blast. THTF wanted to know all about acting and the process of creating a character, and I wanted to know all about his photography and being a DJ. The date went so well that he planned three other dates before we even finished our first one. *Ooo hot damn, this is my jam.*

Call me naughty, but I was still talking to MF even though I said we were just going to be friends. Truth be told, I was hoping he'd put it all together and realize he was acting like a dumbass and that he wanted to spend some quality one-on-one sober time with dis bitch (a.k.a. me). Regardless of my hopes and dreams (yeah, I'm pathetic), I accepted the potential of THTF.

At first, everything was grand, but soon after our second date, I realized just how clingy Too Hip to Function was. But he was such a cool guy that I was willing to overlook the clinginess (...I'm so gracious). He loved music and he was creative, but he was like a gnat when it came to texting and getting my attention. Not only was he always buzzing about in my alone time but he also rarely paid for things, and if he did, it was because we would split the bill. I was telling myself not to be shallow, but as you know, talking to yourself only goes so far before you split at the seams and become crazy.

For our second date, THTF wanted me to meet his best friend and his best friend's girlfriend. We met at a dive bar not too far from his house but miles away from mine. A few minutes behind him, I trailed into the bar where I met more friends than I had bargained for. Everyone was pleasant and had been friends since elementary school, so they were a welcoming bunch. A few stories amongst the group were exchanged, but soon everyone left except for Too Hip to Function, his friend, his friend's girlfriend and me. And that's how our double date began.

Too Hip to Function was perfect, making sure that I was situated and that I had plenty of topics to keep our conversation going. The drinks kept pouring and the night was nowhere near boring. Starting with tequila, then making our way to another bar with mixed drinks and then a final bar with a bottle of wine. I was enjoying myself, except when I began to think how I had paid for nearly the whole night, minus when we split the bill at the first bar, which was like ten dollars each. I pushed the judgment aside and carried on to our fourth and final bar. This time, I didn't drink because the intoxicated me would've probably embarrassed the nice sober me by "jokingly" telling the new fella that he was cheap. Avoiding that hypothetical fiasco, I sipped on water instead and drove him home and then myself.[136]

It was pretty much decided then, I didn't like him, and it wasn't only because he didn't ever offer to pay for me. This night, I learned how frequently he says "babe," which lord knows I hate and, to make

---

[136] Drinking and driving is a no-no and I'm sorry I did it, mom.

matters worse, he wouldn't just say "babe," he would scream it across the room and prolong his enunciation of the only ONE syllable word. *God, why are you doing that?*

To make it truly worse, he didn't know when to cut himself off from alcohol and got piss drunk to the point of me not having a single idea of what the hell he was talking about, he would blame his drunken state on his Native American grandmother's side...*Oh how wonderful. If I want a shitfaced date, I might as well stick around with MF. At least he pays for things.*

So I wasn't sold on Too Hip to Function. He was cute and had some endearing qualities but there was a lot missing. You know those people that you meet and you can just tell that they never take the blame for their actions? You know the type: got too drunk and blamed it on their "shit" day at work, cheated on their wife and blamed it on their parents' divorce,[137] or did too many mollies at a festival because they thought about their dad—the way THTF did.

What I'm trying to say is that THTF was deeply sad but wouldn't acknowledge his sadness. He tried to mask it by being the life of the party and always being the coolest guy in the room, but honestly, when he got to that too-drunk point, he would lose himself to the sadness. I didn't want to deal with a deeply rooted sadness in someone else; I had already dealt with that some years ago with myself and again with some other guys that I had dated in the past. So I knew that I couldn't help him if he didn't want to help himself—and, honestly, I didn't want to help him.

I didn't think THTF was ready. He was still blaming his current state on his father, and I know firsthand how hard it can be to break that habit. I stopped blaming my father for the way I felt (even if some of the things he left us to deal with were shitty beyond belief), and I moved on. What's the point of dwelling on something that you can never change? You accept it, see it for all that it is and isn't, and then you move on to hopefully bigger and better things. Too Hip to Function

---

[137] I know that's extreme but that's pretty much what my father had done.

didn't see the world like that just yet; he still had some growing up to do…a lot of growing up, in fact.

I didn't know how to break it off with him, but I continued swiping my way through matches. Scared of how he'd react to a "break up," I slowly began to distance myself with work and studying my character more in depth. I was scared of hurting this already hurt man, but that didn't stop me from putting myself first (call me selfish…or call me healthy). Eventually, he began to sense the distance, but that didn't stop him from going away for a weekend to some small local music festival (for which I let him borrow my brand new red wig).[138]

I was oh-so thankful that he had left and even more thankful that he said he wouldn't have access to his phone—that gave me time to devise a plan to solidly end things with him. The gods must have heard my cries for help because they blessed me and cursed him with the only excuse that I needed to hear from him to end things. It wasn't until mid-week following THTF's music festival disappearance that I finally heard from him. *No skin off of my nose.*

"Hey, sorry I disappeared," he appeared from thin air.

"That's cool," I texted back.

"I do that sometimes," he wallowed in self-pity.

"Personally, that's not my thing." I had to lay the line.

"I know. I just feel really depressed."

"Why?"

"I took a lot of Molly."

"Well that's why…You know what that does to your brain's chemicals, right?"

"Yeah, I know. I just get carried away."

"That's not good."

"I know but I get caught up with thinking about my dad and the music and I don't know when to stop," he confided in me.

"I really enjoy you but I can't be around someone who struggles with self-control. I dealt with that my whole life with my father and it's not something that I want in a significant other."

---

[138] That bitch never returned it.

My words must not have settled very well with him because I didn't hear back from him for some time, as in weeks. I wasn't trying to be rude, but I was honest. Not using my father as an excuse but an example of what I didn't want in my life. Why would I want to be with someone who was essentially blaming his father for his inability to stop using a drug that would inevitably propel him into a depression after its euphoric effects wore off? That's what my dad did, and it's something I refuse to put up with in my life. I can't control the choices my father made, but I can make better decisions when considering a partner. So my swiping continued.

...

My swiping lead me right to what I thought was SOLID GOLD: Hello Mama's Minion!

At this point, you've all figured out that I'm a sucker for tall, dark and handsome. *Yeah, I'm real original.* Imagine this: 6'3", luscious brown hair, and tan with green eyes...*REPRODUCE WITH ME!!!!* (Just kidding, kind of.) His profile bio said nothing but his pictures were everything. He looked confident and like a complete douche (oh my gawd, it's like we were meant to be). All that was written on his profile was his age and that he had graduated from New York Film Academy. (Wow, imagine what I was thinking now...NYFA.) I sent him my infamous and now-unoriginal message. He responded almost immediately charging me into a happy dance. His response was short and definitely douchey. I didn't care! I was now on the hunt for some smoking hot man meat.

We talked back and forth for the rest of the night but he didn't ask for my number or a date, I was a little confused but not completely deterred. In my mind, he was way out of my league and I was back to my old ways—enchanted by the challenge of an obviously-poor-choice-but-too-gorgeous-to-pass-up type of guy. Oh Dax, will you ever learn?

Later the following day, I logged back onto my account. *He probably asked me out...*Only to find that he hadn't asked me out. *Hmmm, maybe he needs some encouragement?* So, I started up a conversation with him again and, again, he promptly responded. The day wore on, and so did my patience. The entire day had nearly passed, and there I was laying in bed the following night (day two of talking to him), waiting for him to ask me out, and that sexy bastard still hadn't even hinted at it. I kept going back and forth in my head: *Should I ask him out? No, I shouldn't. Every time I ask a guy out or make the first move, they end up not being worth my time...Oh, but maybe he's different? No, I can't. Maybe I should...*

We started saying goodnight to each other and then I decided, *Fuck it.* "Do you want to grab a drink sometime?"

"Definitely! I wanted to ask you," the weasel lied.

So why didn't you? "Here's my number..." I spelled it out for him.

"I'll text you tomorrow."

"Okay. Goodnight." *VICTORYYYYYYYYYYY!*

Hopeful and optimistic as I was, I prayed that he wouldn't be like the putzes I had already gone through on that cursed dating app.

Mama's Minion (you'll come to understand his name in a moment or two) and I couldn't make plans until a week after we started talking. I had a wedding to go to, and he was busy "working."[139] The wedding was on a Sunday, and I knew I'd be too hungover to hang out with him that Monday, so we set our date for Tuesday. Even though the wedding was a blast, I had managed to speak to him for nearly the whole of it. Needless to say, it was an obvious choice for me to drunk call him for the first time when I returned to my hotel room. We had never spoken on the phone before, and I didn't want to make another first move, but I was too drunk and too curious not to call him.

Immediately, I was turned off by the sound of his voice. On his profile pictures (and the Instagram pictures that I had snooped through) he looked so manly and confident, but over the phone, he was soft-spoken and almost feminine sounding. To me, a voice carries a lot of importance, and this guy's expression was timid and measured, almost

---

[139] I still wasn't sure of what he did for work but he had made it sound SUPER important so I assumed he was working on something film-related considering he "graduated" from NYFA.

fearful. Regardless of the sound of his voice, our conversation carried on for some time until my drunken imbecile of a brother and my cousin came crashing into my room. MM and I said goodbye while I was forced to welcome Beavis and Butthead.

Tuesday was upon us, and Mama's Minion had asked me to pick him up from his house for a hike. I agreed, and we set our time for 10:00 a.m. to avoid the sweltering heat that would inescapably engulf us had we gone later in the day. I arrived just before ten to find Mama's Minion sitting on the planter outside of his house only to be reminded that online dating was full of lies.

MM looked nothing like his pictures. He was at least forty pounds heavier, poorly dressed in ill-fitting clothes and a face that advertised his fear of the outside world. *Fuck. That's why he didn't make the first move.* I pulled my car to the curb, he opened the door and hopped in. I acted like I wasn't shocked by his lack of similarity to his pictures. It wasn't that he wasn't a good looking guy, he was a handsome man, but he didn't look the way he had advertised himself online. *Isn't false advertisement illegal?*

He directed me toward the entrance of the hiking trail while I contemplated what to do about my situation. *I was turned off by his voice and now, I am completely turned off by his appearance. Is that shallow? No, that's not shallow. He lied.* I parked the car while he carried the conversation up the dirt road and through the entire (maybe)[140] two mile hike. Somewhere toward the end of mile one, MM's "paddle boarding" back injury flared up and we were forced to turn around.[141] I drove us back to his house hoping to drop him off and carry on my day in solitude, but alas, he invited me in to watch a movie, like we had initially planned. *Ugh!* Being stupidly agreeable, I agreed and once again apprehensively parked my car.

Upon entering his house, we were greeted by the noxious voice of the most overbearing woman I have ever met in my life—MM's mother.

---

[140] That's a very generous "maybe."

[141] He didn't paddle board nor did he surf as he had so falsely advertised. Also, his back wasn't hurting, he just couldn't catch his breath because he wouldn't shut up the whole uphill hike.

She was barely five feet tall but was an in-your-face kind of lady who loved to talk about her chronic pain. Immediately, I was not a fan of her and immediately I knew why MM was so "soft-spoken." His mother was the type of woman who would raise her voice to talk over you if she thought that she knew better than you and, according to her, she knew better than everyone. Almost instantly, "Mama" ordered for her boy to go get her and his little brother a sandwich. He agreed and nearly flew out of the door.

He had told me that he had moved back from New York only a couple months before we had met. Unfortunately, like everything else he had told me, it was a lie. He had been home for some six months, he didn't have a car and he didn't have a job and he never actually graduated from New York Film Academy. I figured out the lack of a car almost immediately when his mother sent him on that secret mission to get her a sandwich and instead of walking to the Audi in the driveway, he transported himself to my passenger door...*Um, I think I should go.* I didn't figure out the lack of a job for a couple of weeks since he always acted like he was "working" but what I later discovered was that "working" meant social media and playing some stupid FarmVille-like game. Everything with him felt like a dead end, yet I stayed with him for nearly four months (three if you don't count the month that I blew him off to go to Europe).

I couldn't wait for our first date to end. His mom made me feel extremely uncomfortable, their dog smelled like the Grim Reaper could come for her at any moment, and MM was not the man he had made himself out to be online. I felt so shallow. All I could think about was how badly I wanted a boyfriend and how it was so hard to find someone with potential that wasn't a complete douche. Well, sitting right in front of me was this kid who was basically pouring his heart out to me about his family and his life and there I was blankly staring at him and consuming myself with myself. I stopped and I started listening, and for a moment I thought I was wrong to judge him and that he was a sweet, down to earth guy. Maybe he was exactly who I needed.

That day, our first date, sitting on his bedroom floor Mama's Minion deleted his Bumble account in front of me and asked me to do the same—and no guy had ever asked me to do that before...So what do you think I did? *God, I need to stop being so predictable.*

I swear, deleting my Bumble created some seismic activity for Millionaire Fuckboy and Too Hip to Function, because all of the sudden, those dorks were barking up my tree again in two very different ways.

My first week of dating MM, Millionaire Fuckboy would call me nearly every night—and nearly every night I would miss the call because I was busy watching a movie, because that's all Mama's Minion would ever do with me. I finally called MF back and he invited me out with him and his friends that Friday. I reminded him that he and I would just be friends since I was dating someone and he said that he understood.

Friday arrived and I couldn't have been happier to get away from Mama's Minion—mostly because I was sick of driving to his house and sitting there all day, listening to his mom bitch and moan about her pain but watch her do clapping pushup challenges.[142] I got out of work early and headed straight to the bar to meet Millionaire Fuckboy. He had been texting me all day, and I wasn't all too sure whether I was making the right choice, so I built out the condition that I wouldn't meet him if he was blacked-out. He swore to me that he wouldn't be (but I should have known that he couldn't help himself). When I walked inside of the bar, I was greeted warmly by a blacked-out MF (by that I mean almost kissed...with lots of tongue. *Grrrr.*) and trailing behind him was some random guy that I had never met before.

Apparently, MF had made a new friend with this rando by telling him to hold his debit card for safekeeping because he had a lot of money. (I wish I was kidding.) All of the sudden this kid was his best friend, and according to MF's new bestie, I was the enemy since all I was interested in was his money. *The fuck did your bitch ass say to me?* In response to this obvious dumbass' apparent mental deficit, I hit him square in the forehead with the palm of my hand and told him, "Fuck off, twat." Rando took a second to realize that I had palmed him and then lunged

---

[142] Yes, she really would. "Oh my effin' back. Doctors just don't get it, they're all idiots." *You just did a shit ton of funky pushups, you nutcase.*

like he was going to do something back to me but MF intervened by taking each of us like baby birds under his wings.

MF and I headed out to the dance floor, leaving Rando behind but without the debit card since I had pick-pocketed it back and forced MF to put it in his wallet. I swear, I felt like his mom telling him to keep his money private. *Who's mommy's favorite Fuckboy? Good boy, now keep your monies to yourself.*

We danced and danced and then MF realized that his real friend was leaving (not by choice, he was being kicked out) so we had to leave too. MF's friend bailed and left him behind. And since MF and Rando were too rowdy in the bar, and we hadn't been served any alcohol since I had gotten there, I was sober (and irritated) as could be. I offered him a ride home, which he gladly accepted (since he could barely tell his ass from his head because he was so drunk).

I drove him to his front door, but he had me park the car because he wanted to keep talking. I reminded him of the no hanky-panky policy. We walked into his house, and he walked straight to his bedroom and laid down. I followed him in to say, "Uh, [MF] I'm leaving."

"No!" he whined.

"I told you I'm seeing someone."

"I want you to be with me," he pouted.

"No, we talked about this. Remember? You were too busy with work." I felt like I was talking to a little kid.

"No. Stay with me!" He was shouting.

"I can't."

"Fine! Leave! Just leave like everyone else does!"

"Hey, that's not fair. We talked about this." I tried reasoning with the little toddler kicking on the bed in front of me.

"I was going to marry you and buy you a house!"

What the fuck. "I need to go."

"Whatever! Leave then."

So I left, and when I tried to ask him if he really felt like that the next morning, he hadn't a clue of what I was talking about. *How convenient.* I never told Mama's Minion any of that, since there was no need to worry him with the dramatics of a drunk.

By week two of dating Mama's Minion, Too Hip to Function was sending me hate texts all day, every day. At first, they were whiny and self-deprecating, and then they turned, well, even whinier and more self-deprecating but with a bit more pizazz because now it was my fault. It was probably wrong of me to never officially end things with him, but I did tell him through text…and it wasn't like we were officially dating. I mean we had gone on like three or four dates in two weeks, which by no means was worthy of OFFICIAL dating status.

I stand by the fact that Too Hip to Function was a great guy, very spiritually aware of the world but also lacking maturity in so many emotional aspects. He would send me these hateful texts, expressing his anger at me for breaking things off with him, and, at first, I wouldn't answer. But finally, I caved when he sent me what I deemed to be my favorite of his aggressive texts: "I'm doing to her exactly what you did to me." What did that mean? It meant that some girl was pouring her heart out to him and he was ignoring her.

First, I would like to say that I never ignored him until he sent aggressive texts. Second, I "ended" it with him because I didn't want to subject myself to someone who may or may not cope with his emotions with drugs and alcohol. I responded with the kindest text I've ever sent and diffused the bomb. It was like it suddenly clicked in his head, and THTF left me alone after that…weird.

So by no means did Mama's Minion and I have a smooth start to our romance (or our pathetic pairing). Each month that we were together, a week before my special monthly gift, I would take a week vacation from him because he would piss me off so badly. (That's not healthy, just in case you were wondering.)

It was always the same thing with him, he'd complain about money and how his stomach hurt and how his skin was breaking out all over his back…I'm not a financial advisor nor am I a medical doctor, but I think that some things are too fucking obvious to never say. No money? Hmm, that's probably from not having a job. Your tummy hurts? Well, I did two seconds of research and discovered that he had a food allergy, which was also why his back was breaking out. These things were so apparent and so easily mended, but for some reason, it was the most challenging thing in the world to him.

Sometimes I felt like I was dating a middle-aged, overly sheltered housewife. I was the moneymaker in the relationship and would have to coax my woman out of the house to go get dinner with me (or the bitch would be difficult and want to stay home to drink a smoothie instead because he didn't want to spend the money[143]). At least once every couple of weeks, I would bail on him for a couple of hours and get dinner and a glass of wine at one of the restaurants down the street. And once a month for an entire week, I wouldn't talk to him because I couldn't handle his bitching a moaning any longer. (Aunt Flo made me do it.)

I felt like I was dating his mother and then sometimes I felt like I was turning in to his mother; hence my week long sabbatical to rediscover what it meant to be an almost single lady, which for me meant binge watching *Shameless* on Netflix and stuffing my face with Mike and Ike candies and attempting to drink an entire bottle of wine all alone. Diabetes and alcoholism have never been so close to me.

I guarantee you've read all of that and thought either:

A.) She's such a drama queen,
B.) She should've just broken up with him, or
C.) Both.

I am a huge drama queen and I thought about breaking up with Mama's Minion nearly every day after our first couple of weeks of dating. But after week two of dating, I felt contracted to him because he said, "I love you." Well—ACTUALLY—he forced me to say it first since he said, "Every time I've said it in the past, it's ended badly, so you need to say it first. You know you want to."

Truth is I didn't really want to say it but I was stuck between a rock and a hard place and had never said it before so I figured: *What*

---

[143] Correction, *MY* money.

the hell. Maybe I'll learn to love him.[144] So I said it—which is why I felt contractually bound to him, which made breaking up with him so much more difficult than it should have been. I should have never fuckin' said, "I love you," because I didn't and there was no way I could.

I think MM knew I wanted to break up with him because he would frequently tell me how heartbroken he'd be if I did. And to be honest, he wasn't the only one stopping me from ending things with him; my mom was too. I'm one to abruptly do things if I feel it in my gut and I've never lasted long in a relationship with a nice guy (because although they aren't written in this particular book, there have been some nice guys in my life).

Mama's Minion was a nice guy; he didn't have a mean bone in his body, but I couldn't spend two days in a row with him because his aversion to ambition was irksome. I felt like my whole life had been a monetary struggle to pay my own way through college and get a car and travel the world because Mommy couldn't afford it and Daddy was a deadbeat. But Mama's Minion was completely content living off of his stepfather and his (tyrannical) mom's disability checks. He boggled my mind and not in a good way. He was miserable, but too scared to do anything for himself, and I didn't want to be miserable and scared. I was and wanted to be happy and adventurous. I needed to break up with him and it wasn't like my reasons with other guys in the past (you know, for being a cheater). The only action that Mama's Minion got from other women was from stalking his ex-girlfriend's Instagram account. It was ridiculously annoying, especially when he would bring up some picture she had recently posted randomly in conversation...*that* pissed me off. That was about the extent of the action he was getting and it was pretty pathetic.

So, Mama's Minion didn't have a whole lot going for him. He was tall, handsome and smart but he was lazy, insecure and fearful. The real irony of dating him? I was annoyed by Too Hip to Function's lack of ever paying an entire bill, and this kid, Mama's Minion only took me

---

[144] That was stupid. The only things you can learn to love are cats and country music...they both just kind of grow on you.

on one date the entire time we were together because he barely had a hundred bucks to his name. In fact, during our date, I was scared that the forty-three dollar bill was too expensive for him to pay.

Why? Why did I stay with him? I don't know. Maybe I thought that I would learn to love him, or that he would eventually find a backbone and stand up to his mom, or that I could change him for the better. I hoped that one day Mama's Minion would be confident enough not to freak out when some ladies were staring at him while we were out in public, "Do you see that?"

"See what, [MM]?"

"They keep staring at us."

"No, they're staring at you," I corrected.

"They need to stop. It's making me uncomfortable."

"You realize they're staring at you because you're ridiculously good looking, right?" I tried boosting his confidence.

"They need to stop. Do I have something on my face?"

"God, *you* need to stop."

I prayed that MM would actually get a job...anywhere. Then I considered paying for him to go to Europe with my brother, family friend, and me, but quickly reconsidered the inevitability of never being paid back. So I left for Europe in July and returned in August only to break up with MM a week after being home.

I felt bad for ending things with Mama's Minion because I felt like he would forever be stuck where he was. A small part of me felt even worse for never being able to help him, but you can't stay with someone just because they're broken and lost (I had learned that already from some other guy—or lots of other guys). I wasn't broken or lost, but he was making me feel like I was.

I literally walked out of the relationship. Mama's Minion said something, and I gathered my things and walked out of his house knowing I would never return. As I walked out, of course his meddling mother stood in the door to watch me leave and shouted, "What's going on?!" *None of your business, crazy lady!!* I ended it and blocked MM on all forms of social media and had my family do the same because I didn't want him obsessing and talking about me to a future (ex) girlfriend like he had done with the girl that came before me. He would be my last Bumble experience. No questions asked.

Then I left a week after for an impromptu trip to Guatemala to mend my mourning heart at a wedding with my favorite player, Rambo. Ah, who am I kidding?! I wasn't heartbroken.

I returned home from Guatemala after only being gone for five days. The trip was the perfect cherry-topper to the long-sought ending of my defunct relationship. Spending my days drinking and exploring Antigua Guatemala with my bestie was the most paradisiacal prescription I could think up to soothe my (unbroken) heart. I met a few Latin gigolo types while out there, but quickly came to my senses and saw them for all that they weren't, so I left them alone. My mind was made-up: I was done with the dating thing.

TG

What is love?

Saturday, September 24, 2017. It had been less than a month since I had ended things with Mama's Minion and no more than two weeks since I had returned home from Guatemala as a newly single and uninterested-in-dating woman. It was morning. I was percolating to the brim of my brain with caffeine and sugar after downing a Vietnamese iced coffee (the coffeehouse equivalent of crack cocaine).

Surrounded by fifteen-year-old National Charity League girls and their bored, house-ridden mothers (since my own mother had generously volunteered us to set up for a charity event), I reveled in the annoyance and caffeine pulsing through my body. It wasn't the end of the world, but it wasn't exactly where I wanted to be. I was at the peak of my caffeine high and spazzing out because the little girls worked too slowly for my liking. And then, I heard it, from across the arena, "Woo hoo, sexy ladyyyy!" I knew that voice and I knew that it was directed toward me. I looked up and saw my friend's mom gallivanting my way.

Pushing past the other half-twit mothers like a linebacker clearing a path for her soon-to-be-victorious quarterback, I knew that a grand ole time was about to unfold. This woman, the one trucking through the plastic bodies of Orange County housewives, is always the life of the party and knows everyone and anyone that you should know. Not to mention, she knows more eligible bachelors than a matchmaker could ever dream of knowing. That being said, Life of the Party ALWAYS had someone that she wanted to set me up with. Well, today was no different than any other day, for on this day she had the "perfect" guy for me.

"Oh, you are looking hot today, baby!" She squealed, slapping my ass.

"Not as sexy as you, mama. Meow," I gave her a little growl.

She busted up laughing and then, "I have the PERFECT guy for you," she cooed.

"NO! No more guys. I'm taking a hiatus."

"No you're not. You're too hot to take a hiatus!"

I rolled my eyes and then of course, "Hey, [Mama]! Isn't [TG] perfect for her?" Life of the Party shouted across some people to a woman I had never met before.

"Oh, my [TG] is wonderful," Mama answered back with her bright blue eyes seeming to sparkle at the thought of her wonderful son.

Immediately, as if my life depended upon it, Life of the Party grabbed me and introduced me to Mama, TG's mother. *Great, I really wanted to meet his mother.*

"[Mama] this is Dax and I want to set her up with [TG]," LOTP winked and nudged.

"Hi," I blushed.

"Oh, so you'll be here tonight then?" Mama asked.

"No, I have plans to meet up with my friend in L.A. tonight."

"You're no fun," Life of the Party whined.

"You know, [TG] used to live in L.A.," Mama declared.

"Oh, really?" I cited, uninterested.

"He's in the film industry," LOTP baited.

"Cool," I assured.

"Yeah, he went to LMU and finished with a Film and Business degree," Mama clarified.

"Really? I went to school in L.A. We must've been university neighbors," I was trying to steer the conversation away from the mommy setup.

The two women dazzled me with a few more details of TG and once again tried to persuade me to stay for the event, but eventually we parted ways and my mother and I drove home.

I will admit that I did look up this TG character that they had spoken so highly of, and I will also admit that I thought he was cute. But doggone it, I was determined to stick with my vacation from men. And since I had been on a traveling spree for the past couple of months, I had this confidence in my self that I had never had before. I felt like I could do anything, be anything, go anywhere and everywhere and be comfortable and content in who I was and what I had done. And I now knew and felt that I didn't need a man to make me happy or to do things with. I could do these things all on my own.

As my mother got ready for the charity BBQ, I didn't regret my decision to not go. I had plans to go to L.A. a little later that evening— but then, right after my mother left, my friend called and canceled our plans. *No big.* So, I made dinner and binge-watched some show on Netflix.

When the clock struck ten, I was deep into my dirty T.V. affair when my brother yelled up to me from our living room, "Hey, Dax!"

I paused my show, "What?!"

"Can you pickup mom? I'm her DD and my friend wants to go out!"

I thought about it for a second and decided, "Sure."

"Cool, thanks," my brother yelled once more.

"What time do I have to get her?"

Silence from the bottom of the stairs.

"PEONNNNNNNNN!" I screamed.

"What?!" he answered, as though he was annoyed. (Some nerve that kid had.)

"What time do I have to get Mom?"

"Uh, now."

"What the hell is wrong with you?!" I roared as I slammed my laptop shut and flung myself out of bed.

"My bad," he moaned as the door collided shut. *Bang!*

So, it was a Saturday night in September and I was now the substitute DD for my mom and her friend. My hair was frizzy[145] and I hadn't bothered to put makeup on since my sole obligation was to

---

[145] If you say "efrizz" then you can speak Spanish.

chauffeur a pair of drunks (a.k.a. my mom and her friend). I had thrown on whatever clothes were on my bed and I didn't think twice about it since it really didn't matter what the hell I looked like.

I parked my car and walked up to the only group of people left at the party, "Mom, are you ready?"

She drunkenly swayed, "Oh, honey, you could have done your hair."

I rolled my eyes but they were startled straight when Life of the Party cut in, "Let's meet some boys," she hiccuped.

"What are you wearing?" my drunk mom whined as LOTP pulled me away.

"Whatever was on my bed," I blasted back, finishing my eye roll.

Life of the Party guided me through the sea of drunks which just so happened to be the only group left at the BBQ. We wove past faces that I knew, faces that I didn't know and faces that I was about to know. She stopped me in front of a man I recognized from his Facebook pictures—sandy brown hair, bright blue eyes, and a sideways smirk—TG.

"[TG] this is Dax. Dax this is [TG]," LOTP slurred. "You're both wonderful," she continued.

"I'm better," he snarked.

"My ass." I shot back.

"Your ass?" he questioned.

"Yeah, with a face like that," I pointed, "it's obvious that my ass is better."

"Oh," he laughed. "You're a big talker, aren't you?"

This continued for quite some time as Life of the Party laughed and looked on, satisfied by another "match" made. TG and I patronized each other with witty, belittling banter, but there was a sweetness to the patronization. I could see the flirty fire in his ocean blue eyes as I hit him with my words and I could feel my cheeks turn rosy from his backlash. TG *was* wonderful.

But then—someone grabbed his arm and they swirled away onto the dwindling dance floor, and just like that, he was gone and I put myself back in check with my abstinence from the male species, gathered my drunk ducklings (my mom and her friend), and we left. But this time around, there was a nagging in my head.

Through my entire drive home, I debated whether or not I should follow him on Instagram, and then I considered messaging him. I was flabbergasted as to why he didn't ask me for my number. There was no doubt in my mind that he had been flirting with me and I definitely had been flirting with him, so why didn't he ask me for my number? But then it hit me: *he's probably a player.*

I pulled into my driveway still debating what to do. Even after sitting with TG's Instagram page open in front of me, my finger hovered over the pestering "FOLLOW" button. I couldn't help but deduce that there had to be something wrong with him since he hadn't asked me for my number. Long story short, my finger cascaded against my phone's screen. I "FOLLOWED" him. And again considered messaging him, but was quickly reminded of the unsuccessful circus ring of guys that came before him. I had made the first move with them and romantic, good times had not ensued. *No, I am not going to message him.*

I left it at that—I followed him—but under no circumstance was I going to message him. So, I double-clicked my home button and exited out of all of my apps and sent myself to bed. *Good night and good riddance to TG.*

Morning came and the afternoon went and Sunday flew by just as fast, and no message from TG. I gave up. And then it was Monday. I opened Instagram, a few notifications popped up, but it was the red circle encompassing the number one that caught my eye. I had one message, and I couldn't help but hope that it was from TG. I clicked on my messages and there it was: a perfectly bolded, unopened message from TG.

TG: "You're so dramatic with your 6 hour late arrival ☺."

Me: "You saucy little minx, you."

"I was fashionably late…not so fashionable, mostly just late."

"Plus, no one wanted me at their table."

TG: "Ya you did kind of smell a lil."

"So are you some kind of charity crasher? Taking advantage of drunk dudes late at night as they are on a natural high…"

Me: "Ew!"

"I showered."

"I washed my hair for you."

"Isn't that enough???!!!"

TG: "Honestly, I kinda like a woman's natural scent."

"Please don't shower because I'm taking you out tomorrow night."

"I know you're an actress, and I'm speaking at a panel at SAG tomorrow night in L.A."

Do you see that?! He didn't ask me on a date; he told me we were going on a date and that was hot.[146]

Me: "Whoa baby…had to break for a victory dance."

"I really need to shower though."

"I just finished two yoga classes."

TG: "Nope, no way. A deal's a deal."

Me: "Cut a dirty girl a break!"

"What time is it at tomorrow?"

TG: "Pretty dress and stanky pits."

"We need to be in West Hollywood at 6:45."

"Where do you live?"

I gave him my address, and added,

"At home still."

"No stank pits."

"And how dressy is my dress supposed to be?"

I typed in my phone number, along with a casual "That's my number, in case you needed it or something." And then he texted me.

Tuesday arrived, and I drove myself to his house from which he drove us to L.A. I was a tad nervous, but for some reason, I still had it in my head that the date wasn't going to go anywhere. I guess I figured we'd go on a date and maybe date for a little bit and then I'd get over him or he'd get over me. I mean, that had pretty much been the accumulation of my dating experiences, so why would TG be any different than those other guys? That sounds horrible, right?

Much to my surprise, our first date was PHENOMENAL! We got dinner at this hip, vegan restaurant. (Yes, I know what you're thinking, but I promise it was delicious.) Then we went to the SAG (Screen Actors

---

[146] Paris Hilton circa early 2000s…that's hawt, so hawt.

Guild) Panel where I sat in the audience and watched him as he spoke about filmmaking. Once the panel wrapped up, TG asked me where I thought we should go next, to which I suggested Mesa, my favorite lounge in Costa Mesa. He agreed and we made our way back down to Orange County.

Shall I preface that Mesa is the lounge that I suggest to all of my dates? I know it, it knows me, and I am bound to run into someone I know if a date takes a turn for the worst and I need an easy escape. You want to know something embarrassing? TG called me out on it right away. "I bet this is the bar you have all of your dates go to since you know the doorman," he coyly shouted over the music. *Am I that transparent?*

I chuckled and told him, "If only you could be so lucky." We laughed and left it at that.

Some time deep into the hour and house music bass, TG asked me, "Why acting?"

I answered him by telling him how much I love writing and constructing the backstory for my characters, "I feel like it gives me insight to so many people, why they are the way they are."

Then, he reached across the void to put his hand on my leg. I jumped back! I didn't mean to; it was an involuntary reaction. His touch was electric. Quickly, he recovered by telling me of a short that he had been working on and how he thought I would be perfect to help him write it and star in it. I agreed, and we went down the rabbit hole of writing that I love so much.

Our drinks ran dry and then it was time to go. TG drove us the couple miles back to his house. We shared music and a few more laughs along the way and then the car parked. I walked to my car and he hugged me goodbye. He didn't even try to kiss me...just hugged me and told me he'd talk to me soon. It was there—that moment—that I deduced that he just wanted to be friends or business partners or whatever the hell that hug was all about.

Three days later TG and I met at my favorite coffee shop to discuss what I had come up with for the short script. I grabbed our coffees and scones as he held down our table. We talked about the few ideas I had, and he told me of his. Mine were complicated and his were simple. (Go figure.) Our brainstorming concluded as we finished our coffees and once again, he hugged me goodbye and once again, we left it as just that—friends who do business (not friends with benefits). I drove home and got ready for work that night.

It was some time toward the end of my shift when I checked my phone and saw that I had a text from him, "I'm coming to the restaurant."

Whoa, no. I didn't want him to see me in my work uniform! I was wearing kitchen Crocs, for god's sake! TG couldn't see me like that, even if we were just going to be business partners. I quickly typed out: "No, don't come. I am getting ready to leave," which wasn't a complete lie.

Milliseconds later my phone lit up with his response: "Too late, I'm already here."

Fuck. Within seconds he walked into the front door of my restaurant. There I was in ill-fitting slacks, a sauce-stained button-up, and a vest with a missing button. But of course, my run-down dishwasher-friendly shoes were the cherry on top. *Ugh.* I tried to hide from him but he spotted me almost immediately. He nodded my way and sat himself at the bar with room for one more—me.

I closed out the last of my tables and took a seat next to him. We ordered drinks and a snack. Our first drink went down with ease and a mellow conversation of our career and life goals, but by the time we were halfway through our second round, he laid it on me THICK. "You know, you're hard to read," he said without looking up from his drink.

"I am?" I laughed.

"You're standoffish," TG interjected my jesting.

I stared at him as he continued, "I'm thirty-two, and I don't have time to play games. I want to get married and have kids one day. If you're not into that, then that's cool, but I like you and want to know if you feel the same way." He stopped and looked up at me, "If you don't feel the same, I'd still like it if we could put this aside and still work together on some projects." He said it like he was scared of me denying him.

I just kept staring at him. No guy had ever been that transparent with me, and he took me by surprise. I had most definitely misread him.

DAX MARIE

The embarrassment of my vulnerability rouged my cheeks as my lips mouthed some words to ease his nerves. Looking back on it, I probably said something that made me seem like I was confident in admitting I liked him but on the inside, I was dying and thinking of all of the ways he could hurt me.

I know what you're thinking, you're thinking that I just admitted a few pages ago how confident I was myself. But you see, that was a confidence to be alone, to face the world on my own without anyone by my side. I didn't know how to be in a functioning relationship, I had only been in ones with emotionally unavailable guys, and the truth of it was that I was actually emotionally unavailable, too. Why was that? I was terrified to get hurt, to be emotionally attached to a man, to let someone know the deeply sensitive side of me. I was guarded and had been for a very long time. But now those defenses were slowly crumbling because this guy, TG, called me out on it.

TG closed out our tab, and we walked out of the restaurant together. He was floating while I felt like I was sinking after telling him that I wanted to be with him. And then, he did the unthinkable—that cheeky bastard grabbed me and planted one right on my lips.

"No!" I pushed away, "Our first kiss can't be in my Crocs!!!"

He looked down at my ugly-outfitted feet and smacked another one onto my lips. I laughed and kissed him back since I knew he wasn't going to stop.

A few days later we had our second official date, and a few days after that we had another, and then another, and then another. Truthfully, I was still unsure if I was ready to be in a relationship and I was still guarding myself. I remember telling myself to keep going, that I was just insecure.

The sureness came two weeks later when we made love—we didn't fuck, we didn't hookup, and we didn't screw around. It was intimate, passionate, gentle and caring, unlike anything I had ever experienced. But sadly my insecurity stuck around. All I could think about that next morning when we woke up was that I needed to get out of there. It was all I knew how to do and all I could hold myself accountable to and hold him responsible for—nothing past leaving. How pathetic is that?

190

The first two months of our relationship were an uphill battle with myself. Everything between TG and I was organic and magical. He listened, talked, shared, kissed, created and dreamed with me, but silently, I was drowning in my thoughts. Continuously thinking the worst of the worst-case scenarios to end us. I felt like I was waiting for something terrible to happen, for it all to end. I just kept rolling with it because I didn't want it to end but there was this insecurity deep inside of me that kept telling me the time would come.

On November 6, 2017 my head shut itself up when I realized that I loved him.

We were sitting on a boat, gliding through the harbor. TG's whole family piled into a tiny electric Duffy boat with us. Everyone loud and shouting and drunk as drunk could be, but in that loud and public moment, I looked up at him talking to his dad. The pinks and oranges from a fading fall sun lit up behind him. He looked so pure, so devoted, so happy, and like gooey peanut butter, "I love you" oozed from my heart to my brain. I held my breath for a second at the thought and I felt my eyes tear up. This was real. This was love. This is what I was supposed to feel.

I wanted to tell him right away, but something inside of me told me that it was too soon, so I held those warm, gushy words in my mouth for three more months until TG said it on Valentine's Day (my first and best Valentine's Day ever).

Our first year of dating flew by, relatively unhitched—that is, until he decided to make a very large decision without me.

Picture this: me happily in love with TG and TG utterly obsessed with me (because we're in love, duh), and then TG goes on a boys' trip. A week later he returns and, while we're hanging out at his house, I invite him to watch my sister's soccer game since she's in California from New York. "I can't," he said.

Bitch, why not?

Then he tells me that he is going to look at a house with his BFF in Venice. Yes, as in Los Angeles, as in seventy miles away from where I live, as in there is traffic and I have a full-time job that I hate in Orange County, which means I can't just go up whenever I want.

I didn't say anything. I just stared at him, that hard, plotting-your-death stare. I figured TG would catch on. He didn't. *Whatever.* Anyway, back to the story...That was strike one: TG—my boyfriend—didn't even hypothetically consider me in his plans to move away, and then he didn't catch on that I was an itty bitty bit upset.

Well, a few weeks pass by, and TG didn't say anything else about this house in the land far away. Everything carried on as usual between us with absolutely no mention of this faraway land. Then, THAT GUY did it, again. STRIKE TWO.

"Oh, baby did I tell you?" he said nonchalantly as I packed my things to go to work.

I stared at him, thinking that he was going to tell me about the crazy deal he had gotten on camera gear.

"I got the place in Venice..."

What the literal fuck.

"I move in October first."

Don't you dare blow up here, Dax. You wait and you go home and think about your actions.

*Insert my head exploding here.

• • •

So, what did I do?

Well, the past Dax would have just stopped talking to TG, and the present Dax (hi, that's me) considered it as a tempting option. But then after crying and screaming and soliciting help and empathy for my grand ole problem from everyone I knew (except TG), I began thinking about it all, about him, about me, about us. And for once, I thought about everything I had to lose if I lost him. TG isn't just some guy. He isn't this guy or that guy; he's *The Guy.*

If I were to end things with The Guy, I would lose my best friend, my confidant, and the greatest and only love of my life. Don't get me wrong; I was pissed (and I'm still a little bitter about it all). I felt abandoned and disrespected, as though he didn't hold me on the same pedestal that I hold him. So, instead of abruptly ending a year-long relationship, I decided I would talk to TG about my feelings. And, of course, he was STILL oblivious to it all (because unfortunately, men don't think like women do).[147] He had absolutely no idea that it was "such a big deal." *Uh yeah, you're just moving away and we're always together, you nut job. Of course it's a big deal.*

TG heard me out (yes, even through my dramatic crying and screaming)[148] and he apologized. We talked about everything we could do to make our situation better.

"Maybe this is extreme," I said, wiping tears from my cheek, "but I would do anything for you and our relationship."

"Gross," he smirked. "But if it makes you feel better, I would do anything for you, too."

So, it was decided. I quit my job in Orange County (which I loathed) and I found a part-time job in Venice to focus on finishing my book and spending time with him...TG, The Guy, my guy.

---

[147] It's an unfortunate, yet necessary evil of the world.

[148] I'm not a psycho, I'm just a passionate person.

Some Words of Wisdom

Only true psychos can psychoanalyze themselves—that's me!

A wise teacher, Mr. Anderson, in a wise book called *The Perks of Being a Wallflower*, once said, "We accept the love we think we deserve." I had never given those words much thought past their context in the book. It was just a poetic line in a beautiful story that summarized everything about the protagonist's life. But it's not some simple line in a novel; it's the truth: we accept the love that we think we deserve.

For years, I had been the girl who thought all men were assholes. If I met a hot guy, he was a cheater; if I met a nice guy, I would walk all over him; if I met a hot nice guy, his ex-girlfriend would magically reappear, and they would ride off into the sunset together. (It's happened twice…I really hope they didn't get sunburned.) I didn't have faith in any men, but now looking back at it, I didn't have faith in myself either.

I could sit here and blame my father for never being there for my siblings and me. I could say that his absence caused me to seek approval from men in my dating life. I could argue that the men that posed more of a challenge to me and were less likely to be attained by me were the ones that I desired more since that's what my relationship with my father had conditioned me to do. I could pinpoint that the year that I lost my virginity and went "loose" with men was the same year that my father let me down the most, and I consequently cut all ties with him.

Maybe it was because I raised myself on the romantic misfortunes of *Sex and the City*, *Grey's Anatomy*, and *Californication*? Maybe it was because I always fought against love and never for it? Or maybe it's as simple as I never thought I deserved a two-sided selfless love? Could it be that I just lacked the confidence to give myself wholly to someone and take the good, the bad, and all of the ugly that comes with that?

I'm not blaming my father nor am I blaming my mother, but the way in which you are brought up has a lot to do with the way in which you see the world and yourself. After all, my father left my mother with three children for his secretary. We were five (me), three (my brother) and six months old (my sister). My mother had no job and depended on my father for money. He decided when and how much he would give her monetarily and he was cruel and controlling. When I was seven, we lost our home because drugs got the better of my father and his money and his business. By then, my mom had gotten a job and was able to get us a shitty apartment, but it wasn't long before we lost that too. Then we moved in with and soon lost Nana, and once again we were left in a shitty financial situation that carried out through the rest of my teenage years.

Growing up was not easy for my small family. But come to think of it, is growing up easy for anyone? I mean, none of us are born understanding this complicated world. We all have to figure it out the hard way. All of us suffer—some just a little, others a lot—but it doesn't matter how or how much, it's what you make of your suffering. Do you fall trap to the same things that affected your dad, the drugs and alcohol? Do you dwell on your hatred and frustrations of your upbringing? Or do you see the faults and challenges of your past and rise above them?

I didn't learn until much later in my life (as in "I'm twenty-five" later) to trust my gut when it came to dating. Hell, I'm still learning to do this. Believe me, this takes work, and it's not something that you gain overnight. Not only did I have to learn to trust myself but also to trust my partner. This trust holds the fate of a relationship. I couldn't love anyone for real because I couldn't trust myself—but more importantly, I didn't think I could trust them. In the past, I always held the boys I dated to such low standards, just waiting for them to mess up, and they always lived up to my expectations. That was on me.

I never thought that I would find love because I never realized until recently that I wasn't looking for love, I was looking for some far-fetched idea of romance that I carried in my head. And romance and love are two entirely different things. To me, love was romance, so I didn't understand why I never got both. In fact, it took me a while to realize that romance is part of the courtship of cultivating and maintaining the *zsa zsa zsu* of love. Romance is a noun and love is a verb (and I need verbs in my relationship…lots and lots of action. *Grrrrrrowl*). I think I found my forever but only because I finally figured out that I was the problem, not just the men that I dated.

Here's what I now know about myself: I fake a hard exterior, I am extremely judgmental of men, and I dwell on things like there is no tomorrow. All of these are fronts which, in the past, kept me from getting hurt—or so I thought. In hindsight, I still think all of my previous relationships would have failed because I chose guys who almost guaranteed that outcome. The promise of eventual failure was my safety net because it meant I didn't have to open myself up too much. Truth be told, I don't think I would have ever realized that I was the problem without someone (well, someone special) pointing out that I was standoffish.

It's too easy to fall back into old patterns, and sometimes I have to remind myself that the only imperfections in my relationship with the most perfect man in the world are the wild thoughts I have. Sometimes I still lack confidence in who I am and that what he and I have is real and that it doesn't matter what has happened to him or me in the past. All that matters is who we are when we're together and MY GOD, he's complete magic to me.

He makes me laugh and cry and scream with joy (and occasionally anger). Of course, we aren't always perfect. We fight and on occasion we frustrate each other, but that's the fun of it, isn't it? Knowing that I love an imperfect being and that he loves me, another flawed human. Trusting in our relationship, which is far from perfection but someway, somehow everything will always be perfect for us if we make it so.

(You can barf now if I'm too in LOVE for you.)

I am madly in love with this guy who for years has slipped past me without me even knowing. Often I've wondered whether we would've matched as well as we do now if we had met before I ran myself through all of those other dull little boys. Honestly, I don't know if we would have.

It took me a long time to find The Guy, but it took me just as long to find myself and truthfully, I don't know if I would have been mature enough without all of my past experiences to accept TG's love. He's wonderful and magnetic, but I don't know if we would have what we have without everything I had to experience and realize for myself before him. I don't know if I really would appreciate him without every pestilent thing/person/self-induced nuisance that paved the path for TG and most definitely matured me.

See, there are no rules to love, and that's why it can be so hard for someone who has never known what love can be to understand that love is imperfect. Love is real, and it's just as messed up as you are. Who's to say that your haggard, disastrous self isn't a shining beacon of light to someone else?

How do you find love if you've never loved? Find yourself, know yourself and know who you can be, and know that you are worth it. For so long I thought that I knew myself but I never knew who I could be and I never knew that I was worth it—worthy of selfless love from another human being.

And that's the craziest part of all of this. I, Dax Marie, am in love. A real-life love that tickles my tummy and makes my heart flutter. And it started with me. I had to learn who I am and know that I am worthy of everything I want, especially a great love. And so are you. Hell, I hope all of my dead-ended ex-lovers find their greatest loves, too.

Be patient my friends and remember to have fun along the way because you are worth a selfish love from yourself and a selfless love from another.

Happy discoveries!

Printed in the United States
By Bookmasters